REACHING OUT TO LONELY KIDS

REACHING OUT TO LONELY
KIDS

A GUIDE TO SURVIVING AND LOVING THE CHILDREN IN YOUR NEIGHBORHOOD

A Revised Edition of *Nobody's Children*

Valerie Bell

ZondervanPublishingHouse

Grand Rapids, Michigan

A Division of HarperCollinsPublishers

Reaching Out to Lonely Kids
Copyright © 1994 by Valerie Bell
All rights reserved

Requests for information should be addressed to:
Zondervan Publishing House
Grand Rapids, Michigan 49530

Library of Congress Cataloging-in-Publication Data

Bell, Valerie, 1949–
  Reaching out to lonely kids: a guide to surviving and loving the children
in your neighborhood / Valerie Bell.
        p.   cm.
  ISBN 0-310-40541-6
  1. Church work with children. 2. Caring—Religious aspects—Christianity. 3. Child care—Religious aspects—Christianity. 4. Neighborliness—
Religious aspects—Christianity. 5. Bell, Valerie, 1949– . 6. Children and
adults—United States. I. Title
BV4647.S9B45 1994
259'.22–dc20   93-33913
                                                                CIP

Cover design by Tammy Johnson
Cover photo by Tom Braak
Edited by Linda Vanderzalm

Printed in the United States of America

94 95 96 97 98 / ❖ DH / 10 9 8 7 6 5 4 3 2 1

Dedicated to the countless children whose silent loneliness has motivated me to write, in hopes the adult world will recognize your needs and compassionately embrace you with belonging.

Contents

Introduction

This is a hard book to classify. Where do you stock it on the bookstore shelves? I have decided that this is a love story, a book to be placed right among the romance novels. True, it may not be the standard Romeo-Juliet, boy-meets-girl, love-at-first-sight love story—but it's a love story just the same.

It is set in a typical American neighborhood, a neighborhood where mothers and children live together—for better or worse. It begins with one mother who is preoccupied with the job of raising her two young sons. Enter a neighborhood of children. Mother meets children, but it's not love at first sight. It's more like repulsion.

Slowly, almost against her will and surely against her better sense, a change begins to take place in this young mom's attitudes. To her surprise, she discovers her heart is roomier than she had imagined and the neighborhood children more lovable than she had first thought.

I must be careful not to give away the plot at the outset, however. Welcome to my story. I hope you will feel the love with which it is told.

ONE

The Kool-Aid Mom

The mamma where I love
says I am a new sance.
I think it is something grown-ups
don't like to have around.

Opal Whitely
written between the ages
of five and twelve

Sometimes we aren't the people we imagine ourselves to be. Take me, for example. I always thought I was a lover of children. As a teenager I was an eager and busy baby-sitter. In college I had no doubt that my major should be elementary music education. A few years after Steve and I were married, I would teach during the day and spend my evenings enthusiastically involved in his youth ministry. I birthed our two sons with extreme joy. All these signs would indicate that I was a pro-kid type. But after my own two sons were born, I realized an ever-widening gulf between my feelings about my own kids and my feelings about other people's children.

In fact, I began to face my real feelings about other people's children when Steve and I, along with our two sons, Brendan, then six, and Justin, three, moved back to my hometown of Wheaton, Illinois. I thought I was a lover of children, but it took the children of Prairie Street to show me the difference between polite tolerance and compassionate caring.

With our move from Florida to Illinois I was able, for the first time in our eleven years of marriage, to quit working and be a full-time, at-home mother. I looked forward to a less-demanding lifestyle. But I wasn't ready for Prairie Street.

Prairie Street was a kids' paradise. More than a dozen children under eight years old lived on this block-long street. The entire neighborhood was their turf. Backyards spilled unfenced into each other, encouraging unhindered play for the length of the entire block. The roadway was theirs too, and they unapologetically held up the occasional traffic with their street games. I learned to look out for my refrigerator and my cookie jar because Prairie Street children didn't recognize the concept of private property. The unspoken rule was "feed one, feed all." Traveling as a pack, they could wipe a family out of food faster than a swarm of Old Testament locusts.

The children talked tough, and among them the pecking order was clearly defined. Mild physical violence was common; occasionally the air would ring with childish screams. All the kids outfitted themselves with the standard Prairie Street survival equipment: a big wheel (for quick get-aways), a large stick (the weapon of choice), and a wad of Big League Chew (completes the tough-kid image).

Brendan and Justin loved it!

But I wasn't so sure. I felt I couldn't relax for a second. Even when I limited my parental interference to times when it was a matter of saving life or limb, I still felt like the neighborhood police mom. I began to experience feelings of nostalgia for the good old days when I was a school teacher.

Then I would tell kids to do something, and they would do it. On Prairie Street they would look at me as if God had just confused the languages at the Tower of Babel, or they'd say something endearing like, "You're not my mother. You can't tell me what to do!"

Added to that frustration was another disturbing development; our house was becoming the place to come and spend the day. Our yard was becoming the gathering spot, the watering hole, the gravitational center of preadolescent social activity. I soon realized that my life was getting to be just like that of the friendly looking woman in the television commercial, the woman who calmly sits in a backyard stuffed with hyperactive kids, all the while passing out Kool-Aid with, of course, a big smile.

A Kool-Aid Mom is the woman who ends up with most of the neighborhood's kids most of the time. The smile and the Kool-Aid are optional. (Now, you are probably nodding your head, thinking—that's me too. I'm the Kool-Aid Mom around here. Well, lucky you! And you thought you'd never win anything!)

Looking back on those days, I now realize it was a situation I managed only to tolerate. Other mothers were less hospitable to my children than I was to theirs, and occasionally, I felt abused. Was I becoming the sucker Christian mom who was too easy to take advantage of? Did our town have some kind of underground information system that has passed out the word about our house? Where did all these kids come from? In my more irrational moments I suspected people were rounding up children from all over town, loading them on buses, and dropping them off a block from our house!

I had ambivalent feelings about so many children invading my private space so regularly. If I stepped in the bathtub and immersed myself in water, I could be sure the phone or doorbell would ring. If I tried to nap, I would be awakened by little hands pounding on the door and little voices calling to me, "Valerie, Valerie, you home?" Although I felt silly about it, I found myself sneaking snacks to my own children so I wouldn't have to feed the whole group. Interacting with this children's world often left me struggling to like myself by the end of a day.

While I was learning to accept my new role, my husband, Steve, and I decided that we wanted to have another child. (Looking back I think we must have been crazy! Why would we want another child when we were already drowning in them?) But you know what we wanted. We wanted another Bell baby, a genetic link to us, another child of our own. The months passed, bringing disappointment and no new baby. So it didn't surprise me when one night I had a dream about wanting another child. In it I told my story to the Lord. Hannah-like, I reviewed my case. I reminded the Lord that we had been waiting a long time, and while I had his ear, I requested that if he could arrange for us to have a girl, we would all be so thrilled. The Lord listened patiently to my story and then quietly asked me, "Valerie, have you looked on your front porch lately?"

In my dream, I rushed to look on the porch. I was anticipating something really spectacular—something possibly wrapped in a pink blanket and sleeping in a little basket. When I flung open the front door, there was a dark-haired boy sitting on the steps. I knew he was not my child; he didn't have the trademark dandelion hair. Still something about him seemed familiar.

"Oh, *that* little boy. Why he's here all the time!" I responded.

Then in a way that made me think the Lord doesn't waste many words, he asked me, "Then why don't you ask him inside?"

I couldn't think of a reason why I hadn't invited that little dark-haired boy inside. "That makes perfect sense. I don't know why I didn't think of it before." And then, faster than is possible in real life, I hurried to bring him into the house. When I did, I was overwhelmed with a rush of joy. I knew the feeling. I had experienced it twice before in my life. It was "bringing-home-the-baby-from-the-hospital happiness." It was "new-mother ecstasy." It made me want to cry and laugh at the same time. The feeling was so intense that it woke me.

"Sure was an unusual dream," Steve agreed as he left for work the next morning. "Maybe there's something to it." He didn't laugh, as I thought he would. And now I couldn't easily dismiss it either. I couldn't shake the impression that lingered—or the residual joy I was still experiencing.

But the ringing phone soon shook me from my thoughts.

"Hello! Jason Andrew's mom? Oh, hi! Yes, we have been seeing a lot of Jason these days. Nearly every day after school, he's here . . . Oh, your divorce is final, and you've gone back to work? I see. You're concerned about Jason?" That's what I was saying, but what I was thinking was this: *Now, why are you concerned about Jason? He's just the biggest little trouble maker around. If there was a junior Mafia, Jason would be in charge of recruiting and training the hit men!*

Our talk continued. "A conference at school with his teacher? He got all A's in academics? Wow, that's super! And he's flunking in his deportment grades? (You know what I was thinking, right?) Yes, I agree that's serious. I don't blame you for being worried about him. What's that? . . . You think he'd be so much better off at my house before school every day instead of by himself after you leave for work? (Long pause). Linda, I want to be honest with you, I can't plunge into this one without thinking it through. May I call you back tonight?"

And as I hung up the receiver, I found myself saying aloud, "Oh, Lord, Jason's hair isn't that dark, is it?"

So my conflict began. Would the Lord communicate to me in a dream? It certainly had never happened to me before. The joy had faded. I was resistant to these unusual spiritual possibilities.

I reasoned that my dream was merely coincidental. After all, my "little-kid tolerance" was nearly used up. I groaned at the thought of having to cope with another child during the hectic pre-school rush. I was tired of being the nice Christian "mom in residence." Living on Prairie Street had given me an overdose of children. "How nice do I have to be, God?" I complained. "I'm not interested in being a saint!"

I was a wrestler, a struggler, and I strained to defend my time, my energy, my turf. I rationalized. I claimed myself the victim of unfair tactics. I had nearly defeated my dark-haired opponent. I had nearly run the unwanted intruder out of my life. I had nearly declared myself the victor when I considered the possibility that I was not struggling against a flesh-and-blood antagonist. Could my opponent be not just a little dark-haired boy but someone more imposing? Could I be Jacob in an apron using my human strength against God?

Sometimes in order for the Lord to bless us, we have to lose the battle. "Bless me!" we cry, "Oh, bless me, now!" But the route to blessing sometimes requires that we lay aside our reasoning, our defenses, our self-interest. We must stop defending ourselves against our Lord and submit to his holy, alien ways.

I wondered what the Lord saw in that little boy. I knew what I saw in him. I saw him as a daily after-school inconvenience. I saw him as a discipline problem, a potential bad influence on my kids. I had been polite but perfunctory in my treatment of Jason. Perhaps, I had hoped, in time he would wander off to some other home and give me some space.

Jesus, however, could see things I overlooked. He saw past Jason's behavior, past Jason's tough-kid exterior to a frightened and frustrated child. He understood Jason's sense of abandonment. The Lord knew divorce had left Jason's mother with few emotional resources for her young son. This young boy was living on emotional leftovers, scraps from the ruins of adult lives. The desperate unhappiness that had caused his home to break up was crushing the heart of this sad boy.

I couldn't see these things in Jason yet, but I knew what the Lord wanted me to do. All the love I had been reserving for that illusive, future Bell baby—the one with the familiar dandelion-colored hair—all that love was no longer to be kept in reserve. I was not to hoard my love or be selective in whom I loved. I was not to love only my flesh-and-blood children or those whose parents came from my social group. I was not to love just the well-behaved children and the ones who would be good influences on my own children.

I was to love the ones the Lord would bring to my home. I was to love Jason. I was to love the snotty-nosed and raggedy-dressed, the uncared and untended, the bossy, pushy, sneaky, grabby, dirty, whining children. They were to be welcomed and received into my heart. I was not to leave them on the porch; I was to open my home and receive them as my very own.

Jesus cared about the children of Prairie Street, and he wanted his love expressed to them. He wanted children who had known early heartbreak to feel his comfort. He wanted to establish a place where he could give them nurture and care. He would begin to teach me how he saw these children. In time, he would love them through me.

Like the disciples, the adult world tends to see children as an ever-present demand or inconvenience, but Jesus says, "Let the little children come to me. Whoever welcomes one of these little children in my name, welcomes me." That is now my everyday privilege.

I learned that it wasn't enough simply to tolerate being the Kool-Aid Mom. I must also convey a sense of welcome. I believe Jesus sees a great need among America's children. His recruitment tactics, in my life and in the lives of others I've heard of, indicate how deeply he feels that the needs of children must be met. It's not enough simply to love our own children, for other people's children whom he greatly loves are hurting. He needs his family of believers to extend love to even those little ones who don't bear our family names or resemblances.

He wants us to provide his love wherever we find need or neglect or abuse. I am learning to administer his special care that says, "Even if no one else has the time for you right now or if no one else can look out for your development, I will be interested in you."

I'm learning to greet the steady stream of children who have turned our backdoor into a turnstile with a welcoming smile. More and more this is not a discipline for me but the way I actually feel. I'm learning to be inclusive instead of exclusive, to put that extra plate on the table more often. I'm learning the importance of asking children questions about their views and their lives. I'm learning to be available to talk while I'm cooking our evening meal or working in the yard. Other people's children are becoming a bigger part of our lives and are affecting more of our decisions; "We must finish off the basement so the kids have a place to play. We need a larger vehicle that's more practical for hauling children."

I pray for these extra children in my life. I find myself worrying about them. Occasionally I hurt for them. With a certain amount of amazement I realize I'm protective of these children who are not of my womb. I care deeply for someone else's children, the children brought to me not by birth but by the Lord.

Even though the every-morning routine with Jason never materialized, he became a regular fixture at our house just the same. The Lord tested the sinew of my spirit, the depth of my love, and measured me by my willingness to do the unusual for him. Learning to care for other people's children has been a spiritual journey through which I'm sensing the Lord's pleasure. I know he approves whenever I'm meeting the need of some child on his behalf.

Having Jason as a regular extra child has been a mixed blessing. It hasn't always been a time of ecstatic joy. Sometimes I was tempted to throw my hands in the air and say "enough already!" I've grown more keenly aware of my basic selfish tendencies. I regularly have to reaffirm my conviction that a child—any child—is more important than my private space. But, I can also see how far Jason has come over the years. This is potentially one great kid!

I've wondered how many other children I've left on my front porch over the years? Were there others who dragged their sad loneliness to my doorstep, but I overlooked the telltale signs and refused them access to my heart? Had I not heard their sad question because of convention or insensitivity? Jason was the first not-of-my-womb child whom I tucked into my heart with an awareness that God was doing something special in both our lives. With sadness, I think of others who left my house as empty as they came. I didn't understand they were looking for a soul mother. I didn't know I could be "mother" for children other than my own. I was unaware, so unaware.

I anticipate a future time when I will stand before the Lord with other believers who have loved other people's children—other Kool-Aid Moms and Dads, Grandpas and Grandmas. He will call us to receive our special spiritual inheritance with these words, "Come, you who are blessed by my Father. For I was hungry, and you set an extra place for me at your table. I was thirsty, and you gave me Kool-Aid. I was a self-care child whom no one wanted around, and you took me in. I was lonely, and you gave yourself to me. I was parked on your porch looking for love, and you brought me in with joy."

We who have loved other people's children will respond, "But, Lord, when did we ever see you in our homes?"

And we will hear these amazing words, "I tell you the truth, whatever you did for one of the least of these, you did for me."

I will remember Jason then, the first "least of these" in my life, through whom the Lord expanded my heart and my vision for children other than my own. And I will remember that dark-haired boy with fondness and wonder, marveling at how God works in our lives.

That dark-haired child has been my house guest for several years now. The friendship between Brendan and Jason has remained intact through the years, despite their very different personalities. In fact, Brendan takes a certain pride in Jason's innate street savvy and ability to play the tough guy when necessary.

"Ma, you should have seen Jason at school today. He was awesome! Some of the tough kids were picking on a little guy after school, just waiting for the chance to pound his smart mouth in, but Jason stood up for the kid. He planted himself in front of that skinny brat and told those other toughs, 'If you punks want to hurt this little kid, you're going to have to take me first! We'll see how tough you are when you have to fight someone your own size. And don't forget, I have friends!'

"I didn't know what to say, but Jason knew exactly what to do. He just took charge and saved that kid's skin!" Brendan reported admiringly. Pride glowed all over my gentler-by-nature son for his backyard ruffian friend, now promoted to knight-on-a-white-horse, save-the-skin-of-obnoxious-little-kids defender.

I suppose Jason will always be drawn to the fray, but he doesn't need to be ashamed of the role of school-yard protector. It requires a certain personality with a high degree of courage and pluck—not to mention a particular sort of compassion that champions the underdog, no matter how smart-mouthed and obnoxious that potential victim might be. There's a place for the Jasons of this world—sometimes we even call them heroes.

As for Jason and me, well, ours is a unique relationship. Sometimes he calls me "Ma," just as my own sons do. It's usually done in teasing as they enter or leave the house, and he chimes in parrot-like with his good-byes or hellos as the case may be. It's said with a naughty-boy twinkle in his eye.

I smile to myself when I realize that I'm not Mom or Mother to this male trio. I'm "Ma." It's a name that carries a certain earthiness. It fits a woman who's occasionally bare-footed and laughing, a woman whose hair is out of place and who always forgets where she's left her keys. What it lacks in dignity it makes up for in comfortableness. If it doesn't ring with authority, it certainly has the cadence of friendliness.

He calls me "Ma."

I rather like that even though I know he's just teasing me. "Ma"—it hints at the irresistible wonder that continues to captivate me; it's closer to how I feel than I would ever have thought possible or than the dark-haired porch-sitter may ever realize.

TWO

Some Friend

*The stranger who dwells among you
shall be to you as one born among you,
and you shall love him as yourself.*

Leviticus 19:34 NKJV

If it took a little dark-haired boy to break the ice of my heart, I guess it's fair to say that a little girl kept it thawed—my persistent friend, Molly.

In *Charlotte's Web*, the children's classic by E. B. White, an unusual friendship forms between a young pig named Wilbur and a spider named Charlotte A. Cavatica. At the beginning of the relationship, Wilbur watches Charlotte eating a fly and thinks, *I've got a new friend, all right. But what a gamble friendship is! Charlotte is brutal, scheming, bloodthirsty, fierce . . . everything I don't like! How can I learn to like her?* Wilbur would soon learn that under her cruel exterior, Charlotte was a tender-hearted friend who would remain true to the end. He would realize that Charlotte was "some friend."

This unusual relationship between Wilbur and Charlotte reminds me of my relationship with my neighbor girl, Molly. Molly began prying her way into my life when she was a five-year-old. Red-headed, chubby, with freckled apple cheeks,

Molly could win the Campbell-soup-kid look-alike contest. Opinionated and bossy, she constantly treads the thin line between precocious and obnoxious. As I came to know her, I often thought that by some freak of nature Molly was actually a forty-year-old woman trapped in little-kid skin!

By the time she discovered me, Molly had already burned her bridges with the children on the block. But Molly was resourceful, and she found a way to cope. Her typical routine was to knock on our door and ask if our two sons, Brendan and Justin, could play. I soon realized that this question was simply a formality. Her real intention was to shadow me everywhere—talking, talking, talking.

I never had to wonder what Molly thought about anything; her opinions were infinite and free. Given to philosophizing, Molly gave unsolicited advice on areas such as menu planning ("avoid saturated fats"), the apparent maturity of little girls compared to little boys of the same age, and wardrobe building in the "correct" colors. "Gauche!" she dubbed one combination I was considering. She was right; I decided against it. Molly and her opinions were omnipresent and inescapable.

Having a neighbor's child like Molly constantly in the home tests a Christian's commitment to the believer's sovereign placement in the world. After all, Scripture does say, "God ... determined the times set for [people] and the exact places where they should live" (Acts 17:24, 26). *It sure would be nice just to close the door some days without experiencing guilt,* I often thought. When we're lights in the world as Christ commanded, we may be "bugged" by the persistence of the ones who are attracted to that glow. Like a moth battering itself against a screen to get to the light, this child, I realized, would do anything to be with us.

There was no getting away from Molly. Most afternoons she would return from school, drop off her backpack at her house, then follow my boys through our back door thirty seconds later. Perhaps she sensed my ambivalence at the inescapable elements of our relationship because in time she developed a new tactic that was hard to refuse. She learned that the "open sesame" to my back door was, "Got any housework I can help you with?"

So what if she locked the boys out of the house after she mopped the kitchen floor? Even Brendan and Justin could see that was preferable to having to do the floor themselves. Her tendency to take charge made her the first to answer our phone. Okay, sometimes she would go a little too far by screening all my incoming calls with, "Valerie couldn't possibly come to the phone now. May I take a message?" Even the President of the United States couldn't get through her self-appointed protection system.

Slowly I learned that even a pushy, bossy, little girl has her good qualities. Molly was great at our boys' birthday parties. Her authoritative voice couldn't be missed, and when she barked, "To your corners, men!" wrestling would stop, bodies would disperse to chairs, and the party would continue, under considerable direction and control.

When Molly was ten I began to understand why being in control was always so important to her. Her home is both modern and secular. She was more familiar with women's liberation than salvation. Her mom had a career with an hour commute each way to her job in the city, and her dad was living with his new female friend. Molly's alone much of the time.

Molly was a latchkey kid, or to use a more descriptive term, a self-care child. Molly looked out for herself.

I began to see that Molly wasn't just filling up time at our house. Molly was filling an emotional and spiritual gap in her soul as well as she could. She was trying to take care of Molly. She would hang around our family table, even if she had already eaten, just for the talk. "You mean you don't know about David and Goliath?" my boys asked incredulously.

"Uh . . . no," she responded.

What's this? Was there really something about which Molly had no opinion and about which she knew nothing? Then the "experts," the Bell boys, launched into the story, acting it out, hamming it up, with fanfares and flourishes until Molly knew the entire Scripture story.

She loved it!

Something else she loved was listening to me sing church music. Perched in my living room, she would record my practicing on her little Fisher-Price tape recorder for playback at bedtime. No one had ever taught Molly about the soothing comfort of speaking to God in prayer. When this child lay in a dark room at bedtime, she had no spiritual reassurance against death or broken homes or nuclear war. Molly's spiritual needs had been neglected. I sometimes wondered what fears, insecurities, and desires reached Godward when Molly listened to my music in bed at night. Our family was the spiritual "salt" in Molly's life, and she had a tremendous thirst.

She began to insist that her family attend church. When they appeased her by attending one in which the highlight was Barbie doll Sunday (when the little girls would bring Ken and Barbie to Sunday school), Molly was unimpressed. "Actually, between you and me, Valerie," she shared, "it's not much of a church at all. We hardly ever talk about God!" I couldn't help wondering where this little girl's spiritual perceptions came from.

Even now, my relationship with Molly still consists of filling in some of the tangible gaps of a self-care child—picking her up at school when she's missed her bus, bandaging the wrist she sprained in a fall when her mom wasn't home, doing her hair in a last-minute ponytail before a special day at school.

But there's a gap in Molly's life that concerns me more than these functional areas. She's spiritually neglected—and wide open to whatever comes along. How can unpraying parents teach a child to pray? What kind of love sends a child into the world without spiritual resources to cope with the inevitable tragedies of life?

Children seem to be very much aware of God. They naturally lean toward spiritual life. But millions of children like Molly make the spiritual journey alone, unguided, and in hostile environments. These children are given no spiritual resources to cope with the loneliness and tragedies of their childhoods. This is the saddest form of neglect I can imagine.

We neighbors talk on the phone and on the sidewalks that link our houses on Prairie Street. Molly's mom says her daughter has picked up a "quaint little habit" of praying. "She's praying that she'll make a new friend at school. She's praying for help with her homework. Where does she get this stuff?"

I say, "Molly's a spiritually inclined child. She has inside her an emptiness that she's seeking to fill. I hope she'll fill it with the right things."

Her mom says, "Well, we're not spiritual, that's for sure. She's just not like the rest of us. I don't know what to do about her."

I say, "If Molly keeps spending time at our house, she'll pick things up. You know she's welcome, but you should know we pray at our house. We talk about spiritual things."

Her mom says, "Well, I guess it's okay for this stage of her life. She'll probably outgrow it anyway."

And so it goes, our living with each other on Prairie Street.

Yes, I understand how Wilbur the pig felt about his un-usual friend Charlotte. *Oh, Molly, to think when I first met you I thought you were obnoxious and pushy! Molly, you are not only some child . . . but some friend!*

No one loves me as Molly loves me. She dropped in one Saturday morning a while back. You never have to wonder what Molly's thinking. She took one look at me and said, "You don't look so good."

"I'm not feeling very well, Molly."

"Then you should go to bed!"

For some reason, I did as directed. *Yes, Ma'am, General Molly! It's hard enough to stand up to your strength of character even when I'm feeling well.*

Later that afternoon she came back, announcing, "I'm here to fix supper." She managed to produce a chili supper served in our best china with candles and cloth napkins. And why not—she had snooped in my cupboards for years and knew where everything was.

Molly. What a kid. What a friend. I hardly have an adult friend who loves me as Molly loves me. Some friend!

Opening your heart to another person's child can be a precarious thing; Wilbur would say it's a gamble. But it's a gamble that, if you take your chances, may make a positive difference in one of these children's lives.

I realize I will not motivate you by simply quoting statis-tics, because you and I both know that dealing with real flesh-and-blood children is not an easy matter. You may ini-tially react to these children by wondering if you can like them, much less really care for them.

Admittedly, self-care children are rarely model children. But opening yourself to such relationships can yield great rewards. Children like Molly return love in full measure. They've learned to have minimal expectations from the adult world. They won't require much of you. They may follow you around talking your ears off or simply hang around just wanting to be with you. The truth is, however, that most of these children can be easily integrated into the patterns of life in your home.

I don't stop my routines for Molly. If I'm cooking, I give her a job. The other day while we were working in the kitchen, I listened to her word choice. "Do *we* have any flour?" she asked. When Molly's with us, she's home.

"Can we stay for supper?" she asked the other night after she had helped me prepare a big pot of chili. She and I both knew we had enough chili for herself and her friend, so I had no excuse. A little reluctantly, I put aside my plans for a quiet family supper with just the four Bells. I denied my desire for a little private family space. Molly set two extra plates.

"Anyone want to pray?" Steve asked.

Molly's hand went up. We bowed our heads, and she prayed a simple prayer that made my eyes fill with tears. "Dear Lord, thank you for this food. And thank you that we have a place to come to. Amen."

I looked at Steve, my understanding spouse, this husband who is my co-host to Prairie Street's children. I thought of all the times these children have been under his feet or lying on our bed watching television and eating crackers when he got home at night. His eyes met mine. He too had heard the words and understood.

Molly had picked a "place to come to" where prayers could be heard, where her spirituality was affirmed, where she would have company on her journey toward God. Molly's empty space was being filled with believing. When that filling is complete, she will never again be truly alone. That is something Molly need never outgrow.

THREE

Bless the Beasts and the Children

Because of little children soiled,
And disinherited, despoiled,
Because of hurt things, feathered, furred,
Tormented beast, imprisoned bird,
Because of many-folded grief,
Beyond redress, beyond belief,
Because the word is true that saith,
The whole creation travaileth—
Of all our prayers this is the sum:
O come, Lord Jesus, come.

"Come Lord Jesus"
Amy Carmichael[1]

American children are waiting. They conduct a vigil while adult debate whirls around them. They are waiting for voices that will represent their best interests. Small and powerless, they need champions to take up their cause.

We are living in times of unprecedented changes in family life, and these changes have significantly affected the American child. Change begets change, and sweeping transitions are in the wind—solutions that speak of reform. These shifts are meant to address the growing concerns of the American family.

Whether or not you have children, in time, you will be called on to participate in decisions that will affect the future of American children. We must be very careful to base our choices on the right criteria. We must be sure these decisions reflect not only what is best for the adult community but also what is truly best for children; failure in either area would be the ultimate tragedy for children.

Just think about some of the families you know—in your neighborhood, your circle of friends, your church, your relatives, your acquaintances. What lifestyle changes have they experienced in the last fifteen years? Undoubtedly some of those families have been broken by divorce. Others have had to make adjustments because the mother has gone back to work for a variety of reasons. Many families are struggling to find their footing in the midst of these changes.

Most of the debate in the midst of these changes has been centered on our adult concerns. Women, in particular, have felt the stress and confusion of some of these societal shifts. The stay-at-home mom may sense that her lifestyle is devalued in today's society. Just pick up any women's magazine; if the stay-at-home mother isn't totally ignored, then she's presented as the dinosaur of the decade. Though her inner convictions may tell her she's important, outer influences constantly chip away at her self-worth. The stay-at-home mom struggles to feel that her life is significant and well spent. I'm concerned for her.

I'm also concerned for the working mom. I'm one. As most working moms realize, professional demands must coexist with family concerns. Making sure children are packing decent lunches (when not supervised, my sons have been known to avoid the tedium of sandwich preparation by substituting "quickies" such as raw spaghetti or vitamin pills); laying out clothes (with the traditional clash of opinion about what goes with what); and filling out school forms ("This was supposed to be turned in when? Last week? Oh, brother!")—all these things happen in a concentrated simultaneous blur while I try to get myself out the door and off to work. I fantasize about smooth, organized mornings in the same way that other people dream of tropical islands. It's not easy being a working mom.

But even the stress of mornings isn't great when compared with the guilt many working mothers experience over leaving their small children in someone else's care. This is a hard dilemma for most working moms, and they have shed many tears over it in the past decade.

Adding to the despair of working mothers are the voices that insist all mothers should be home with their children, regardless of their individual situations. Some of these voices discuss working mothers as if they were a new phenomenon. Actually, we've been around at least as long as that Hebrew superwoman from Proverbs 31. In the midst of the debate about working moms, I'm glad the Lord held up the Proverbs 31 mother as a model to emulate. Here is a woman who developed her family skills and her personal abilities simultaneously. She reminds us that the working mom's attempts to develop her abilities and interests into cash for the family, all the while juggling child-rearing, are nothing new. It might be a fast-paced jig, but it's not a new dance step!

More and more Christian women are hoping to "dance well" and someday win the Proverbs 31 mother's double blessing of praise from her family and praise for her work at the city gate. We, who are mothers, must be careful, though, that our society's preference for praise giving at the city gates does not seduce us from our priority work: that less-praised work of nurturing our families. So again, I'm concerned for the working mom. I would like to help working moms make those hard decisions about childcare on the basis of all the information they need and deserve to have.

We are all familiar with the debate—and with the stone throwing that usually accompanies it. But in the midst of our adult problems, questions haunt me. I can't silence their persistent nagging in my soul. Could we be so preoccupied with our own problems that we've overlooked the problems of children? Are we so busy scrambling to adjust to the shifts in our society that we've failed to understand how these changes are affecting children?

Too often Christian families find themselves responding to neighborhoods that no longer reflect fifties-style family values by wishing they could build a moat and pull up the drawbridges of their homes to shelter their own children from outside influences. For some, the response to change has been fear, self-isolation, and insulation.

But in today's world, where many people want children but so often fail to take care of them, Christian families may find themselves surrounded by lonely children who want to be included in their family life. We must understand that the question is not only, "What's happening to my own kids?" We are on the brink of a major societal tragedy if good people continue to be concerned only for their own flesh-and-blood children. The trend toward home-schooling, affinity play groups, or exclusive church involvement may reflect the trend to insulate and isolate. The questions we must have the courage to ask are, "What's happening to our collective children? Does anyone have a clue about how America's children are doing?"

Unfortunately, when it comes to America's children, the bad news is abundant. Most of the signs indicate that all is not well in the child world. You are probably aware that something of tragic dimensions is happening to children today. We've all seen the "missing" children pictured on milk cartons and at toll booths. Their smiles greet us as bittersweet reminders of young lives subjected to the unspeakable, the unknown.

But are you aware of some of the other signs that indicate the child world is experiencing extreme stress in America today?

Did you know?

- Children have become increasingly at risk in their own homes, at the hands of those they call Mommy and Daddy. Since 1980, reports of child abuse and neglect have increased nearly 90 percent to 2.5 million per year. An average of three children a day die of abuse in our country.[2]
- Family breakup is causing disruption in many children's lives. In a revealing and clarifying piece for *The Atlantic*, Barbara Dafoe Whitehead points to the fact that while "the dissolution of intact two-parent families may benefit the adults involved, it is harmful to a large number of children." This article cites that:
  - One million children go through divorce or separation every year.
  - Only 50 percent of American children can expect to spend their entire childhood in an intact family.
  - Contrary to popular belief, children of divorce "do worse" than children in intact families on several measures of well-being.
  - Children in single-parent families are six times as likely to be poor. They are also likely to stay poor longer. Twenty-two percent of children in one-parent families will experience poverty during childhood for seven years or more, compared with

only two percent of children in two-parent families.

- A 1988 survey by the National Center for Health Statistics found that children in single-parent families are two to three times as likely as children in two-parent families to have emotional and behavioral problems. They are also more likely to drop out of high school, to get pregnant as teenagers, to abuse drugs, and to be in trouble with the law.

- Research also shows that many children from disrupted families have a harder time achieving intimacy in a relationship, forming a stable marriage, or even holding a steady job.

Conclusion? Family dissolution not only impacts children but also "dramatically weakens and undermines society." Divorce is no friend of children. Divorce is no friend of society.[3]

- Of all the children *under six years old* who are living with parents or a parent, nearly 10,000,000 have either both parents or their single parent working. Many of these children spend at least a part of the day taking care of themselves.[4] If that's hard to get your mind around, picture a city the size of New York City totally populated with children under six years old, taking care of themselves. That's what some neighborhoods have become during certain hours of the day.

- In the largest report ever done on how latchkey status affects adolescents, the University of Southern California Medical School found that
  - "Compared with fully supervised peers, kids left alone 11 or more hours a week are twice as apt to feel highly stressed and at odds with parents, and

to believe risky behavior, like breaking rules for fun, is worth the trouble.
- "They're also more likely to consider friends a greater influence on them than parents, experience higher anger levels, and feel greater fear when alone.
- "The more hours a teen spends without adult monitoring after school, the more negative the impact."[5]

■ At least 500,000 American kids are homeless. New York alone has at last 11,000 homeless kids trying to live in shelters and welfare hotels. This is the ultimate kind of "home alone" experience.[6]

One family counselor put it to me this way. The unsupervised hours after school have become to our American teen culture what the back seat of the Chevy used to be.

Something alarming is happening to children in America today. And most of it is happening without a whimper, a sound, or a recognizable complaint from those young victims around us.

A song called "Bless the Beasts and the Children" describes the low status of childhood.

Bless the beasts and the children.
For in this world they have no voice.
They have no choice.

We can easily recognize that children are America's most silent minority group. They have no voice. They often try to protect their abusive parents when they should be screaming for help from someone. They suffer alone; they suffer quietly.

They also have no choice. They have little power. Like beasts, they are easily exploited. They are easily victimized.

Many adults would like to interpret the silence of children as a good sign. But are children doing as well as adults would like to believe? If America's children could break their silence and express their feelings, their fears, and their stresses, would we discover beneath the seeming quiet that all is well? Or would we learn disturbing secrets locked inside that mute child world?

When their childish voices turn adult twenty years from now, what will we learn then about their childhoods? Will they praise us for the nurturing we've given them to carry into their lifetimes? Will generations to come remember our parental era with thankfulness? Or will they shake their heads in dismay over what we've set in motion?

One thing is certain. In twenty years they will tell us what they can't now, but then it will be too late to make changes in their lives. We should be concerned about children not only because they are our future, not only because they will be our final interpreters to a remembering world, but also because they are helpless, totally dependent on the adult world to act for them.

Increasingly it's not enough for me that my own children appear to be doing reasonably well. For some time now I've been haunted by small faces I've never seen and little children I've never held. These youngsters belong to someone else, but their lives are tucked between the statistics and the trends. They are children not of my womb, yet I feel as if they are a part of me. They're loved and unloved, cherished and ignored, protected and subjected to life's cruelties. They're nobody's children and everybody's children. In a sense they belong to all of us. I fear their story has been largely untold—they've had no voice.

Please understand that I'm cautious about raising a red flag concerning the status of children. It's sure to bring adult insecurities and emotions to the surface. If you mention the effects of divorce on children, divorced parents feel defensive. If you mention statistics about the increased number of mothers in the work force, then working moms feel criticized. I'm not interested in placing blame. I am interested in the facts about how children are doing. Beyond the facts, my primary goal is to find solutions to their problems.

What will happen to children if we don't have the courage to ask the questions they can't ask for themselves? Someone needs to represent their interests. Harold Howe II, senior lecturer at the Graduate School of Education, Harvard University, expressed the problem succinctly in a recent speech delivered at a national convention of school psychologists. "Children in the U.S. today are losing ground. The interests of adults are taking center stage, and the interests of children are being pushed into the wings. Who is the champion for children?" [7]

Sometimes when I read the facts and statistics, I'm overwhelmed. Then I remember this one thing, a hopeful thought: Jesus is the champion of children. He has always been the champion of children. He accompanied Margaret Fell, the Quaker prison reformer, into the dungeons of England. There children waited to be hanged. England was used to gathering for such entertainment and placing bets on how long it would take a child to struggle to his death. Margaret, the mother of eleven, worked tirelessly for and won more humane treatment for children. Seventeenth--century England was slow to understand her vision, but eventually she raised the consciousness of many.

Amy Carmichael understood the Lord's concern for children. As a missionary to India at the turn of this century, she dedicated her life to saving children from the horrors of temple prostitution. She modeled Christ's concern for children in a hostile Hindu land. She saved some—and by her dedication inspired countless others who felt the intensity of her vision.

We are at another time in history when the needs of children must be addressed. In a sense, I'm afraid that we are as barbaric to children in our day as were the England and India of past centuries. Even though children obviously occupy the bottom of our societal barrel, their problems are subtle and still hidden to some. It will take compassion and courage to address these needs. I believe the church of Jesus Christ is not only courageous, but responsive and resourceful as well. In times past when the bride of Christ felt his heartbeat, knew his intimate desires, and responded to his concerns, the church led society to creative solutions.

We have that kind of opportunity today. It's time to stop throwing stones and come together. An alarm is sounding in our society about children. Few credible solutions have been posed. Now is the church's moment. It is time for our response.

We may not be able to solve all the problems, but we are not impotent either. We can do *something*. If you've ever delighted in a child, then your heart already knows the way. If a knot has ever formed in your throat over the problems of a particular child, then your journey has begun.

Together, yet each in our own way, we can reduce the problem to manageable size. You and I are the benediction God lovingly pronounces concerning children today. "Bless the beasts—Bless the children." I can't lay down this tune. At times I've tried to silence it, but it keeps rising, demanding to be heard over the cacophony of my life. The children are waiting, so I sing, "Bless the children, Oh Lord; please bless the little children." They need a voice, so my small voice rises begging other voices to join in. My journey requires other travelers if it is to have an impact. I know other stories must be added to mine.

While the children keep their vigil, looking for hopeful signs from the adult world, I sing to you— "Come, love someone else's child with me. Come love nobody's child. Come let Jesus champion the little children where you live. Come and join me in singing the song that pleads our voices. Bless the children. Oh, Lord, please bless the little children. Bless them through you who read my story and understand my heart. Bless them through me."

FOUR

Self-Care Children

Each for himself, we live our lives apart,
Heirs of an age that turns us all to stone;
Still we have something left of that fair seed
God gave for birthright; still the sound of tears
Hurts us, and children in their helpless need
Still call to listening ears.

Owen Seaman
from *"In a Good Cause"*[1]

Becoming sensitive to something means having a height-
ened awareness of its presence. In the case of children's
problems, it sometimes means reading between the lines,
understanding unspoken words, and interpreting signs.

I realized this one evening as our family watched the news
together. During yet another human-interest piece about
children, the newscaster reported about one grade school's
attempts to encourage creative expression in kindergarten
students. I only half listened. The reporter explained that
the children had been assigned the task of inventing ma-
chines that would help with household problems.

The camera showed open-toothed grins of proud little
boys standing next to their own robotic creations that, if

operable, would wash dishes, make beds, and vacuum floors. I didn't notice the other inventions until the camera took a close-up of a little girl. She was holding a rectangular pillow next to her head. Inside the pillow a tape recorder played back the voices of the little girl's parents. "I love you, Sarah!" the recording purred. "I'll be home soon, honey," a voice reassured. The reporter's voice had become subdued by the awareness that the little girl's pillow invention wasn't just another cute idea. A sad story lay behind this child's creation.

My heart took a knowing jump. I knew exactly what "household problem" that little girl was trying to solve with her tape-recorded messages from her mom and dad. Here was a child whose greatest "household problem" was the loneliness she felt when her mom and dad were gone. I wondered how much of the time Sarah spent separated from her parents. I wondered if Sarah was a self-care child.

I know others have developed a sensitivity that mingles with concern. Not too long ago the following letter to the editor appeared in a Chicago suburban newspaper:

> I would very much appreciate you helping me deliver a message to someone from a little guy who can't do it himself.
>
> The other night I left my friend's house to find my car helplessly stuck in the snow. There were two little guys no more than 12 having a snowball fight who stopped to help.
>
> We pushed and pushed but the car would not move. One little guy's dad called him home, and I started to go back in too. I noticed the other little guy looking so sad and alone, I couldn't resist asking him if he wanted to come in and warm up and I'd see if I could scrounge up some candy or pop.

After a short while I asked him if his parents would be worried, and he said they weren't too concerned about him as long as he got in before curfew.

When I said I had to go, he got a sad expression on his face like he didn't have a friend in the world, and I think he felt that he didn't—so mom and dad, this letter is really for you.

Your little boy is desperately reaching out for somebody. That someone is really you, but after 11 or 12 short years, he's willing to accept companionship and attention anywhere he can get it. How long will it be before he finds it with a gang or the wrong crowd or even worse?

The reason I am writing is not just for this one little guy, but for all the little guys and little girls out there looking for a direction to go who have no one there to show them the way.

Sixteen years ago I knew another little guy whose father had passed away. He was a little too big for his mom to control by herself, though she did try. That little guy didn't stop until he ended up spending a little while in jail and nearly throwing his whole life away.

Yes, moms and dads, that little guy was me, and jails, rehabilitation centers, and streets are cold, hard places. After being through that and more than I care to mention, I don't want to see that happen to your little boy or girl.

Listen, I'm not the most savory-looking guy in the world. I have shoulder-length hair, and I usually wear jeans and a T-shirt. How was this kid to know I wasn't John Wayne Gacy?

Is this where that kid belonged—watching a bunch of strangers playing cards and drinking? But he just seemed so hungry for an adult to spend time with him and pay some attention to him that he just didn't care. He was glad to be there.

I saw myself when I was a kid. I looked at him, and I thought, *That could be me.* Don't get hard and beaten down at such a young age. That's what I was thinking.[2]

I have read through many reports and statistics trying to get to the heart of the childcare issue today, but I believe the core of the truth is best captured in this newspaper column excerpt. The writer obviously learned to interpret the signs through his own tragic childhood. For those of us without a "knowing background," this man's letter casts light on the figures and statistics and gives us a window into the realities of self-care as lived out in the lives of many children.

Who are self-care children? Self-care children spend at least part of most days caring for themselves. The term is specifically used to describe latchkey children, but I would like to use the term to describe children whose parents, for a variety of reasons, just "aren't there" for them. A self-care child may have working parents, divorced parents, parents with consuming personal problems, or parents who simply lack the basic nurturing skills necessary for meeting a child's needs.

A large percentage of children falls into this category for one of two reasons: either both parents work away from the home, or divorce has left them in single-parent families. A great debate currently rages over how many American children actually spend time in self-care every day. Census figures tell us that 54 percent of children six and under have working mothers.[3] That percentage rises to 72 percent once a child reaches school age.[4] Other statistics estimate that nearly a fourth of the children between six and fourteen spends part of each day in self-care. That's as many as five to seven million children who take care of themselves while their parents work.[5]

Some interest groups have tried to argue with the accuracy of these figures, citing the lack of differentiation in the statistics between full-time and part-time working mothers, and mothers who work just part of the year, during the Christmas holidays, for instance.

While technically they may have a point, it's important to realize what they're trying to say about the problem of self-care. By claiming the statistics are overblown, some hope to convince us there really isn't much of a problem. And if we don't have much of a problem, they reason, then we don't need government funded daycare.

Sorting through these conflicting figures has left me somewhat suspicious of statistics. Do we have a problem in childcare, or don't we? I've discovered that adult interests have muddied the waters on both sides. The truth undoubtedly lies somewhere in the middle.

I suspect that truth can be found in our own neighborhoods, in the lives of the children around us. When I think of individual lives, I realize the issue isn't whether it's seven million or "only" two million children living on their own— if it's just one little guy living without the adult attention he needs, it's too many. Just one lonely child looking in the wrong places for love (or its easily mistaken substitute— attention) is a potential tragedy.

The question we need to ask is not, "How many children are in self-care," but, "How is self-care affecting America's children?" Some people are beginning to ask that question. Many recent studies have focused on self-care and its effects on children. But even the experts have conflicting findings. Some studies optimistically support the practice. But interestingly, this optimism is usually cited in popular magazines targeted for a working-mother audience.

Some studies have suggested that self-care children actually like being home alone. But Ellen Gray, former Research

Director for the Prevention of Child Abuse, cautions that adults sometimes need the ability to read between the lines. A course offered by the Kansas Committee for Prevention of Child Abuse asks children to complete sentences. The children's answers help determine if they are trained and ready to spend time at home alone. One question, in particular, is designed to find out what information the children would like their parents to provide. "When I'm home alone, I wish I knew . . ." evoked sentence completions that expressed the lack of companionship 35 percent of the time, and most of these responses specifically mentioned parents. This is poignant evidence that self-care children still strongly wish their parents were home with them. Self-care children would like being home alone—if their parents could be with them!

Based on this evidence, Ellen Gray concludes, "The biggest problem for children in self-care is not their fear or boredom but their loneliness. There is only so much that can be done to combat the loneliness of the child in self-care. The findings of this project accentuate that for most children, self-care is no substitute for adult-supervised childcare."[6]

Loneliness is the tragedy that millions of America's children live with on a day-to-day basis. It's not nurturing or love or caring that marks their days, but loneliness. It's the Grinch that's stealing their happy childhoods. Loneliness sends them off to school in the morning and greets them at the end of their day.

I'm a working mom, but I consider myself blessed. My job hours are flexible, so I'm able to adjust my work to my children's school hours. My job is a part-time job—actually a full-time job shared with another working mother who is also a writer. I'm usually at home with my kids not because I'm afraid they'll burn down the house or become closet chain-smokers, but because I want to be with them. I wish my options were available to all working mothers.

Our neighborhood, which once had nearly every mother at home, now struggles to accommodate a growing number of self-care children. These children park on neighbors' porches and backyards out of loneliness. Sometimes I've been insensitive to their struggle to belong; I've been naïvely indifferent to their isolation. But I can't escape this one piece of commonsense knowledge: when the need for adult attention is unmet, children will satisfy that drive by forming attachments with substitutes. Like the little boy in the letter, many children seek to fill the lonely emptiness of their lives. Who will they find to fill the vacuum—people like John Wayne Gacy or like Mother Teresa?

Although many studies have highlighted the effects of self-care on children, they don't address how many parents just "aren't there" for their children. For an increasing number of American children, their need for love and attention from the adult world is unmet. Their ignored need to "be with" may create such a vacuum, their need to belong may be so unsatisfied, they may feel so emotionally detached, that on an emotional level they are really "nobody's children."

It's not enough simply to become sensitive to the enormity of the problems before us. That is the job of the talk show hosts and the media. Instead, we, the church, must move beyond awareness to action. Christian parents need to pray over their children and make adjustments if they suspect they are raising a lonely child. Christian parents need to model responsible rearing of children.

But beyond that basic point, we also need a spiritual surrogacy movement. We need to address the problems of loneliness in the lives of children whose parents cannot or will not provide for their basic emotional and spiritual needs. We need adults who are willing to be the substitutes lonely children need.

I'm looking for certain people—not perfect people—but people who are strong enough to reach out to a child in need. I'm searching for married, single, retired people who have been blessed with resources of love and care and who can give from that mighty reservoir. I'm calling on those who will overlook their own needs long enough to care for children who may be hurting.

I'm seeking men and women who are disturbed by the thought that even one child in their neighborhood goes to bed weighted with loneliness. I believe many of us have the ability to put our arms around just one or two extra-lonely children and embrace them. I'm calling for people who can envision making a difference for the entire community of American children by simply reaching out to one or two little ones nearby.

I'm praying for America's children—for the ones who display the telltale signs of loneliness, the ones who quickly wear out their welcome or become involved in questionable friendships and hang around where there's potential trouble. Sometimes I pray for them by name. Other times I have to say, "Lord, protect that little boy. He shouldn't be riding his bike by himself at this hour of the evening." Or, "Father, that little girl looks so sad. Please touch her life with your special love through someone today."

You can begin to make a difference for children—the ones you know by name, the ones you simply recognize, the ones unknown to you—by praying. Prayer will clothe statistics in the flesh and blood of real children. Prayer will open your eyes to the children nearby and to their needs. Prayer will make you sensitive to the Lord's heart in this matter. Prayer will move you beyond sensitivity to action. Prayer will change things for children by changing you.

FIVE

Are You My Mother?

*We are born helpless. As soon as we are fully
conscious, we discover loneliness. We need
others physically, emotionally, intellectually;
we need them if we are to know anything, even
ourselves.*

C. S. Lewis

The problems of some children are captured in a little
"Beginner Book" called *Are You My Mother?*[1] The plot is simple. A baby bird hatches from his egg while his mother is off
hunting something for him to eat. For sixty large-print
pages, he searches for her. When my boys, Brendan and Justin, were younger, they would laugh at little bird's repeated
question, "Are you my mother?" And why not? It delighted
them to imagine that a bird might think a kitten, a hen, a
dog, a cow, a boat, a plane, or something called a snort,
could be his mother. Eventually baby bird's mother-quest is
satisfied, and the happy ending pictures him cozily snug-
gled in the nest under her wing.

This is a funny little book, but unfortunately, for a growing number of American children with full-time working
parents, the question "Are you my mother?" may reveal the

central uncertainty of their young lives. The feminization of the workplace means more mothers are leaving younger children for longer periods of time. These children are at great risk of going through life without bonding to a primary nurturer. Many of them will not have the tenacity of baby bird. They will give up trying to develop attachments with the adult world. They will grow to adulthood unable to trust or to form satisfying emotional relationships.

For some children this inability to establish a trusting relationship with an adult will result in more than just feelings of rejection or distrust. A frightening body of evidence suggests that in some adults an "unbonded" childhood results in a rage that expresses itself in crimes against society.

One expert describes it this way: "It's as if a voice inside their heads is saying, 'I trusted you to be there and to take care of me, and you weren't. It hurts so much that I will not trust anyone, ever. I must control everything—and everybody—to ward off being abandoned again.'"[2] It seems that the seeds of despair are sown in our children in their infancies, which result in crops that range from detachment to psychopathy.

I am indebted to Dr. Ken Magid and Carol A. McKelvey for their fine work, *High Risk: Children Without a Conscience,* that brings together a large body of research in this area. Magid and McKelvey focus on the threat unbonded children hold over our society if their developmental nurturing needs continue to be ignored. Citing the growing numbers of psychopathic murderers, or conscienceless murderers, they warn that our societal trends that shuffle young children to various and numerous caregivers may be unwittingly creating children whose bonding processes are disrupted, leaving them emotionally handicapped and dangerously detached.

These unattached children are susceptible to becoming time bombs whose names will eventually explode across headlines like Charles Manson, mastermind of the Helter Skelter murders; Theodore Bundy, the infamous mass murderer; David Berkowitz, the "Son of Sam"; and Kenneth Bianchi, the "Hillside Strangler."

We are baffled by headlines about psychopaths who walk into school rooms and kill children, and we wonder at the growing number of children involved in violent crimes against playmates, parents, and strangers. It's as if a horrible sequel to *Are You My Mother?* is being written every day in our nation. Something's gone wrong with baby bird, and he's toting guns and looking for victims. For sixty large-print pages, his life erupts in violence against those who unfortunately cross his path. He has no regrets, feels no remorse.

Experts estimate that the number of psychopathic personalities in this nation falls between .05 to 15 percent of our population. If you take just a 5 percent figure, that would mean out of a U.S. population of 250 million, 12.5 million Americans are possibly psychopathic.[3]

Multiply that figure by the number of people who are not psychopathic, but who suffer a kind of disconnected emotional existence due to poor parental bonding in childhood, and you can begin to understand why many experts are very alarmed about what is being called a "bonding crisis." My concern is not so much the threat that unbonded children hold over society with their potential psychopathy, but rather, the threat our society unknowingly holds over children with our childcare practices.

We have few cures for an unbonded infancy. It seems that very little compensates for that deprivation in our early years. This means that we must, as parents and as an adult community, work very hard at prevention. We must not be satisfied with providing only enough care for children to still grow up okay. We must start asking, "What is best for children? What are their optimal growing conditions? What is the most excellent emotional atmosphere that will encourage health and quality of life?" When an adult society begins to apply those questions to the helpless among them, then and only then can they deservedly call themselves a civilized country.

Just what exactly is the bonding process that must develop between parent and child in order for a child to grow emotionally straight? How can we keep this important process from being interrupted in our children? Bonding is a trust process that begins with birth and develops throughout childhood, particularly early childhood. It teaches children that they are cared for, that their emotional and physical needs will be met, that they have nothing to fear.

The cycle of bonding is easily recognized when a baby is hungry: The baby begins with a *need* (hunger), responds with a *rage reaction* (crying up a storm), that leads to *gratification* (food), and finally, *trust* (the look that says, "Thanks, Mom!")[4]

This bonding cycle is reinforced every time the primary caregiver meets a child's emotional or physical needs. In the food cycle, trust is built every four hours. In the emotional cycle, trust is built much more often.

The bonding cycle encourages attachment. According to Vera Fahlberg, a renowned pediatrician who specializes in emotionally disturbed children, "The bond that a child develops to the person who cares for him in his early years is the foundation for his future psychological development and for his future relationships with others." She lists how that attachment helps our development.

Attachment helps children to

- attain their full intellectual potential;
- sort out what they perceive;
- think logically;
- develop a conscience;
- cope with stress;
- handle fear and worry;
- develop future relationships;
- reduce jealousy.[5]

Magid and McKelvey state it simply: "Attachment is the most critical thing that happens in infancy other than meeting the baby's physical needs."[6]

This attachment may be made with the birth mother, a foster mother or adopted mother, or the father counterpart. But the bonding relationship is characterized by much more than simply meeting a baby's physical needs.

It's vital to the child's emotional development that this cycle be unbroken. The most sensitive time in a child's life for the forming of the bonding cycle is during the first three years of life. Any disruption during these years can be critical for the child. Many things can disrupt the bonding cycle: postpartum depression, illness, divorce, abuse and neglect, prolonged adoption or foster-care procedures, death of the bonding parent, and separation from the primary caregiver by substitute childcare.

Substitute childcare or daycare has a unique place in this list because it is the only disruption that appears as an angel of light, a provider of solutions. It helps the adult shoulder the responsibility of childcare. It's easy to understand why so many adults are singing its praises. But for the child world, it may be a particularly subtle wolf in sheep's clothing.

Staying in daycare full time can put a child's emotional development at great risk. Bonding disruptions brought about by daycare may establish an avoidance-rejection cycle between children and their primary caregiver. Children can learn to protect themselves by rejecting loving advances from caregivers they perceive as not totally trustworthy.

Psychiatrist Peter Barlow and colleagues at the Michael Reese Hospital recently researched 110 one-year-olds. Half of these children were cared for by a full-time parent; the other half had substitute, but stable, care. The substitute-care children had significantly less secure relationships with their mothers. Why? It seems that many infants interpret daily separation from their working mothers as rejection. These children cope by withdrawing from her.[7]

Keep in mind that this study was done on children with stable substitute care. No one knows the additional problems for children in daycare centers where the turnover rate of workers is high and the ratio of child to caregiver is over the recommended three-to-one ratio. We can only suppose that children raised in these circumstances are at greatest risk of being unable to bond to any one caregiver. This is of particular importance in light of evidence that daycare for infants in the one- to three-year range is increasing more than any other group.[8]

And what about the old rule of thumb about quality and quantity time? It now seems that not only is quality time important but quantity of time as well. How much time away from a baby is too much? In the 1970s, Jay Belsky, child psychologist and professor of human development at Pennsylvania State University, was an early advocate of daycare. He didn't believe that it affected child development adversely. But due to his own recent studies and a body of other recent evidence, he has concluded that children spending more than twenty hours a week in care away from their parents during their first year of life are in danger of becoming more insecure than other infants.[9] Belsky's is not a voice crying in the wilderness.

Other studies also point to a disturbing social development among children raised in daycare. The University of North Carolina in a study of five- to eight-year-olds who had been raised since three months of age in "extremely high-quality" daycare found they were more aggressive than other children.[10] This noncooperative spirit was not reserved only for other children. It was also displayed toward parents and teachers. Is this shades of "baby bird" beginning to tote his gun in anger against society? Time will certainly tell. But by then it will too late for several generations of children.

We need to understand that we are dealing with a narrow but crucial window of time in a child's development. Fortunately, recent evidence suggests that children whose moms return to work after their children are school age may do better when their moms work. A broad study coming out of Kent State University shows that children's academic and behavior performances are positively related to maternal employment.

It was not the children of full-time working mothers or full-time, stay-at-home mothers who scored highest, however. The children of part-time working mothers did best. "They were also more successful if their mothers held a high-status job with flexible hours and were satisfied with the dual roles of working woman and mother," concludes John Guidubaldi, project director.[11] This study establishes a relationship between a mother's happy adjustment and her children's adjustment during the grade-school years. It is possible for a woman to work and for her children to do well after the initial crucial years of bonding are established. Timing, it seems, is everything.

But for the first years of a child's life, many experts urge mothers to be very careful. Burton White, former director of the Harvard Preschool Project, advises, "After more than 30 years of research on how children develop well, I would not think of putting an infant or toddler of my own into any substitute-care program, especially a center-based program. Unless you have a very good reason, I urge you not to delegate the primary child-rearing task to anyone else during your child's first three years of life. Babies form their first attachments only once. What's at stake is the basic human capacity for loving other humans."[12]

In the mid-1970s when I was trying to make the decision about returning to work, I had little to base my decision on except a wing and a prayer. Enough time had passed, however, for the results of studies about the effects of working parents on children to begin to come in. It turns out the reassuring advisors who stressed quality vs. quantity of time were wrong. So were the reports' initial studies that concluded that under optimal conditions, daycare was not potentially harmful to children.

We will be hearing a lot about daycare in the years to come. It seems everyone wants to believe it's the answer for our childcare crisis. Undoubtedly there will be much debate over how to provide children with the care they need, many voices raised pro and con for various approaches, a lot of press coverage for various plans and for those who oppose them. But I wonder, in the midst of the debate, are we asking the wrong question? Could it be that daycare looks so appealing because we're asking the question, "What is best for adults?" instead of, "What is best for children?"

It's a fortunate child whose parents will be willing to ask, "What's best for this child?" and then adjust their own life–

styles accordingly. I fear that many parents will find it too easy to believe that daycare, particularly once the government takes the financial sting out of it, is the solution to their childcare problems.

We need a label like the one the Surgeon General puts on cigarettes warning that if you are going to continue smoking, then you may have to deal with cancer in the years ahead. We need a childcare label that would be issued to parents, warning that the use of full-time substitute childcare may be fatal to a child's emotional health in the years ahead. While it's true that not everyone who smokes will get cancer and not every child in substitute childcare will develop the problems indicated in the studies—some will. Just as there is a link between smoking and lung cancer, there is a definite link between substitute childcare and a wide range of childhood developmental problems.

I'm concerned that the bandwagon atmosphere prevailing in Washington may cause the government to provide American children with the very thing they should be warning against. While they assure the American public that they are interested in "raising the quality" of the present care available, I'm uncomfortable when I realize that they have also given us our public school system, much of which is in need of wide reform. Are we to believe that they'll somehow get it right this time? We must be very cautious whenever high hopes are raised about daycare being the answer to our childcare problems. We must prudently inspect any governmental plans offered families in the coming years. Do they address the child's early attachment needs, or do they favor the adult community's needs for custodial childcare? Does the plan encourage the mother who may be able to stay home with her child to do so, or does it reward mothers with incentives to leave home for the workplace?

To whom can children look in their quest for belonging? Who will pick up the emotional slack too often unrecognized by their own parents? The place to look is to ourselves. We who make up the private sector can begin to address this crisis, without congressional funding, without building expensive new facilities, without complicated programs to train teachers in the art of nurturing. We don't need a lot of agency red tape to make this happen.

Thank God for public-school teachers, daycare workers, Sunday school teachers, and youth workers, who recognize the emotional needs of children and who give more than their share of love and professional care every day. But this isn't just a job for the "professionals."

It's a job for any sensitive adult who recognizes when children are asking, "Are you my mother?" It's a job for adults who are "there" with enough time to make children feel that they belong. It's a job for perceptive adults who are selfless enough to ask, "What is best for children?" It's a job for anyone whose heart aches knowing a nearby child feels like nobody's child.

What is the answer to children's problems today? Vera Fahlberg states it well: "A primary person to whom the child can become attached, who responds to the child's needs, and who initiates positive activities with the child seems to be indispensable."[13]

After speaking about the loneliness of today's children and the need for sensitive adults to be there to fill the emotional gaps, I received a phone call from a woman who told me what her childhood had been like.

Her mother was a single parent who worked to support her family, leaving her little girl alone at home. The little girl was too young to be alone, but unfortunately the Christian woman across the street, instead of looking out for her, called the police and reported her mother's "neglect."

The results for this young girl were tragic. Her mother couldn't stop working and apparently had no one from whom she could ask for help. The mother worked out an alternative solution. The little girl stayed home alone, but she had to hide. She wasn't allowed to turn on the television or lights. She wasn't allowed to go outside and play with the other children. Her mother was afraid the "Christian lady" would turn them in to the police again and that her daughter would be taken from her.

What a sad way to grow up!

It's sad not only for the little girl but also for the compassionless Christian woman who could have opened her heart and home to a little girl but instead chose an alternative that brought so much isolation and pain. It's terrible to grow up to be hard and judgmental. Think of it—to know the pain across the street and close your heart to it every day! It's heartless.

That's why I'm encouraged every time I see signs that aware adults are ready to assume a role of surrogate parent or older brother or sister in some lonely child's life. I'm happy for the child, but I'm also pleased for the adult. It may make all the difference in how they both grow old!

SIX

A Heart Visitation

A baby is an inestimable blessing and bother.

Mark Twain

A young mother sits among friends and shares the frustration of her day. Gently, she speaks from her heart. The child next door is unruly. Even as a youngster, he's foul mouthed. He's a bad influence on her younger children. It hurts her, but recently she's had to send him home.

The adult group is sympathetic. They listen. They affirm her actions. They say she has done exactly what everyone in the group would do in her circumstance.

The next time the group gathers, this mother again shares her struggles over her neighbor child. A part of her understands why he is as he is, but another part doesn't want those problems playing in her backyard! But here is the interesting thing: though she sends him away, she doesn't forget him. He returns and camps on the porch of her heart. His presence conducts a vigil, hoping for a change in her attitude. His visitations are made to her spirit. He's a child who won't go away.

This scenario captures the ambivalence adults feel toward children. We can be simultaneously attracted and repulsed by them. We both admire and are exhausted by their energy. We consider their honesty both refreshing and barbarous. Isn't it strange, children are not only the topic of adult prayers but also the brunt of adult jokes?

"I too have an 'extra' child in my life," a woman recently told me. "My son plays with an older neighbor boy who is a bully. He is also a trouble maker, plays with guns, and thinks it's neat to 'pee' on the trees in my yard rather than use the bathroom. He makes rude noises when I ask him to do something. But more and more I am seeing the lonely little boy inside." What can create more mixed emotions in an adult heart than one five-year-old boy?

Unless it's a four-year-old girl. A letter came to me in the mail recently, "Today when I heard you talking about the needs of children on your radio broadcast, a very specific child came to mind. Amy is a four-year-old girl who lives in our neighborhood. To describe her—deceitful, obnoxious, uncultured, no manners. I'm sure you get the picture!" I do, and I also recognize the concern that this adult reveals with this description of such a "model" child.

Christ recognized the adult world's mixed feelings toward children. His own disciples displayed this ambivalence in their misguided attempts to shield Jesus from children. Officious and ever impressed by their positions of intimacy, they established themselves as his bodyguards, protectors against small intruders. They sent away the children who were just a little too dirty, lest they should smudge the Lord's robes. The disciples waved away the loud ones; they were too distracting to those who had come to hear the great teacher. The adult intolerance and bias of the disciples separated children from the Lord.

Jesus must have been appalled. There's a sternness in his words, "Let the little children come to me, and do not hinder them, for the kingdom of heaven belongs to such as these."

Perhaps the disciples even placed their hands on these children to restrain them physically, but just as likely Jesus was addressing the attitudes they displayed. He specifically points out the attitude of adults toward other people's children. He implies that we may be potential barriers between himself and someone else's child. The word that Jesus uses here, *let*, is not just a passive let—a kind of "get out of the way" so children can come to him. But rather it is an active let—meaning release these children. "Do not hinder them" carries the idea of don't restrain them or don't hold them back or don't be a barricade that some child has to get around in order to find Jesus.

I'm afraid most of us are more like the disciples than like Christ in the way we relate to children. We send children away with our adult attitudes, and we hinder children from knowing about God. We construct barriers with our adult prejudices. Many adults think kids just aren't all that important or are too childish to bother with. If only children could just be a little more civilized—as we are! Our intolerance may not be openly hostile, but in other ways that we do not recognize, we probably say, "You're not worth bothering with." Have you ever noticed how common it is for adults to overlook, ignore, or treat children rudely?

Few adults even bother to initiate conversation with children. At our house Steve and I try very hard to teach our children how to speak to adults by asking questions and then responding with interest. How often I've thought someone should teach the reverse to adults.

It's discouraging to see our children stand on the edge of adult conversational circles, unnoticed, unacknowledged. It seems that many adults don't consider children important enough for even a nod or a hello. This kind of insensitivity gives children the wrong message. It says, "You're not important enough even to notice." We need to free children from adult behavior that belittles or devalues them so they can understand their value in the Lord's eyes. We should release children from our prejudice so they can sense God's acceptance. We need to let go of our they're-just-kids biases so we can treat them with the same high regard that was typical of Jesus' behavior toward them.

We need to free children not only from our adult biases but also from our inappropriate priorities. These priorities usually motivate us to construct barriers that keep children out of our space and off our property or away from our children. It's common for adults to keep children at arm's length, hoping to keep the kitchen floor untracked and furniture unsmudged. Having a clean house is some adults' main concern.

Our aloofness shows children that they are unwelcome on our manicured lawns, in our beautiful gardens, and around our children. It's a common tendency to protect private family times from the noise and bother of other people's kids. Some Christian homes function as if their priority is to keep their own personal kingdoms complete with the little princes and princesses they've enthroned in their line of succession. Too many Christian families' coat of arms could read, "Us four and no more!"

I fear many Christian parents are missing the point. It's seductive to think that if all is well within the walls of our home, then we have done our job. The market is so glutted with teaching about raising our own children and keeping the family together that we've forgotten why doing so is important. Preoccupation with the *family* may distract us from the realization that the *world* is falling apart. The reason for our existence as Christian families is not just to be happy families but to be kingdom families. If we're concerned only about building our personal kingdoms, then we will never be the light that points the way, the salt that creates a spiritual thirst in those around us.

Jesus reminds us that other things have a higher value than our orderly private worlds. "Do not hinder them—for the kingdom of heaven belongs to such as these." Jesus understood the spiritual capacity of children. He saw their tendency toward awe and wonder. He held up their dependent, trusting faith as a model to the adult world. Children remind us that we live not only in a material world but also as spiritual beings, capable of unquestioning faith and pure devotion.

Do you feel ambivalent toward a child in your life? Are you keeping a child in your neighborhood at arm's length? Are you holding her or him away from your life and from the Lord?

The Lord addressed my ambivalent feelings in a dream. Maybe you haven't dreamed about someone else's child, but maybe you keep thinking about a certain boy or girl. Who is the Molly or Jason in your life? Maybe you could like the kid if it wasn't for a perpetual runny nose or a disgusting habit. Still, you find yourself thinking about the child.

Someone sent me a newspaper clipping about a Dayton, Ohio, woman who tore down her barriers to meet the needs of the children in her neighborhood. "It all began with a thrown stone," the newspaper clipping begins. "Dianthia Gilmore's four-year-old son was bruised above the eye, and Dianthia was angry. While [she was] apprehending the culprit, it occurred to her that the act of violence was prompted by the envy of a child who saw her children's fenced-in yard complete with its peach trees and lavish toys.

"Instead of retaliating she decided to invite the stone thrower into her back yard. 'I decided I could either teach the children how to get along, or keep my children isolated inside the fence.' Now instead of the rock-throwers being outside the fence, they are inside the fence, playing. 'Once you make friends with your enemies, you don't have enemies anymore.'"[1]

What raises biases in a mother faster than someone else's child doing bodily injury to her own? Yet Dianthia was able to look beyond the behavior to the source of the rock throwing. This perceptive and accepting mother's circle of young friends has grown so that now Dianthia Gilmore has become a substitute mom to thirty to forty youngsters who call her backyard home every day. This is a real Kool-Aid Mom. The article reports that on any given week her shopping list may include a hundred frozen pops, ten one-gallon jugs of fruit punch, and several jumbo bags of popcorn.

The article continues, "Gilmore, who said she didn't keep track of what she spends, said her sensitivity toward the well-being of children came from her own childhood. She grew up in a segregated neighborhood in Virginia, where she learned what it was like to look in at prosperity from the outside.

"'I always said if I ever made it, I won't forget how hard it is.'" So when children come with bare feet, cutoff pants, and insecurity or low self-esteem, "'I teach them that you are somebody; you can be someone.'"

She often talks to the children about going to college, "We have to start with the children and put positive ideas in their heads now. If we don't work with our children, they're going to be the ones breaking into your house and knocking you on the head."

Dianthia Gilmore is a member and teacher at the Open Door Missionary Baptist Church. She is also a Kool-Aid Mom who broke down the barrier of wanting to protect her own children to bring the children in her neighborhood home to Jesus.

I read another story that tells of a couple who put aside self-interest to minister to a child in need. It began, "Last year our daughter started dating a man who was separated from his wife. He had two children. The older child lived with his mother in another state. The younger child, a boy, lives here in our town. We had several 'problems' with our daughter's relationship, . . . the biggest problem being that this man was separated from his wife. The second biggest problem was that he had this little boy in the picture.

"When this man left his wife, he went to live with a friend, but there was not room in the home for a two-year-old boy to sleep, so he came to sleep in our home every evening. He stayed with us for several months, and he continues to stay with us from time to time.

"It really disturbed us to learn that there were times when this little boy was left home alone in the dad's apartment when we thought his father was caring for him. Our daughter is bonded to this little boy though she is not romantically involved with the father any more.

"We have tried over the last year to express love and acceptance to this boy whenever he is with us and treat him as we would a grandchild. We read to him (which I'm sure he doesn't have done anywhere else). We have tried to teach him new things; show him God in nature; give him a happy life when he is in our home. When I rock him to sleep or scratch his back to try to lull him to sleep, I sing songs like 'Jesus Loves Me,' just as I did with our children when they were little. We've started a photo album for him now so he will have something to help him remember the time spent in our home."

When I read that, I wondered if I would put aside my disapproval of my daughter's relationship to reach out to the child of the very man I felt was so wrong for her. Self-interest would counsel against doing anything to encourage the relationship. Yet these loving adults heard and followed another voice, a voice that called them to compassion and care for the child involved.

What prejudices or barriers have you erected to keep children in their place and out of your space? It's time to dismantle your prejudices for the sake of that child who's there every time you turn around. Who's playing Dennis the Menace to your version of Mr. Wilson? Who seeks you out when you're busy with yard work? Is someone little making a visitation in your heart? Have you felt an unexplainable bonding to a particular child? What child in your life won't go away? Part of you says, "Oh, it's nothing," but another part of you senses the persistence of the Lord's Spirit. "Let this child come to me. Don't hinder him or her; I want to do a work in both of your lives."

If so, maybe the Lord is asking you to do a special work in the life of that inescapable someone. Will you consider the possibility that the Lord has brought a child of his choice into your life? Will you open your life to that child who's making visitations to your heart? Will you begin to welcome the child who won't go away? Will you allow yourself to care for someone else's child?

SEVEN

A Lost Art

I am only one, but still I am one. I cannot do everything, but still I can do something; and because I cannot do everything, let me not refuse to do the something I can do.

Edward Everett Hale

Artists have long understood the beauty of the relationship between the nurturer and the nurtured. Mother-and-child is a classic theme that repeats with variations throughout the history of artistic expression. The old masters make the relationship look so easy, so right. Yet being a parent is not as easy as it looks on canvas. Parenting requires so much more than just giving birth to a baby. Knowing how to parent is not something that spontaneously happens when the doctor slaps a newborn into lung-screaming life and declares its gender. Having warm feelings of love toward a child doesn't mean that you will automatically be a good parent. Parenting is an art that must be developed and honed.

Caring for children is one of life's most demanding roles. Nurturing children requires the delicacy of a diamond cutter, the strength of a sculptress, the tenacity of a weaver, and the undying vision of a painter. It's not easy. The raw material—children—are by nature hard to handle, uncooperative, willful. But a well-reared child is beautiful to behold. Diamonds pale and fortunes fade when compared to children who are on their way to making a positive contribution to humanity. If you're good with children, you perform one of the oldest and best arts.

Most people would agree with these values in principle at least, but in reality, they sadly devalue the skill of nurturing children. I fear it's becoming a lost art. Today's applause goes to those among us who have been materially successful or who work in high-status careers. Those who carry on the art of nurturing a child do so quietly, unheralded.

Do we still recognize the beauty in an adult hand lifted with care to dry the tears on a child's face, or does it seem wonderful only when it's been captured in a painting by an old master? Do we see the charm in the face of a young father who strolls in a park with his newborn proudly worn in a papoose sack close to his heart? Do we recognize the artistry in words that chases fears from a child's heart, the skill that turns pouting into laughing, the mastery that successfully handles the public temper tantrums of a two-year-old? Or have our values been so drastically altered that these nurturing skills no longer seem important?

The fact that nurturing is a hard skill is revealed most clearly by the way we have traditionally tried to abdicate this responsibility to someone else. Throughout history it's been fashionable and convenient for parents to hand over the chore of nurturing to others. Before the invention of the bottle, when breast feeding was the only way, those with sufficient resources hired a substitute—a wet nurse to provide nourishment for the child. Then there were nannies—women who oversaw the day-by-day care of other people's children. In the days of extended families who lived together, in a less formal but still significant fashion, a favorite aunt or older sibling often provided nurture care, filling in the emotional empty places left by the parent. History reveals that the hand that rocked the cradle has often been the hand of a substitute.

Other cultures have been much more open to the concept of caring for other people's children than our American culture. This is a strange thing when we realize that these cultures often were pagan, but their values seem closer to Christian than our own do at times. As a Naskapi Indian once told missionaries, "Thou hast no sense. You French people love only your own children; but we love all the children of the tribe."

Occasionally today the world recognizes people gifted in nurturing, substitutes who have opened their arms and embraced a hurting world. Their lives cut across secular values and model saintliness to us. The media have rightfully extolled Mother Hale, an older woman who turned her New York City home into a nursery for babies born with drug addictions. We admire her efforts to comfort babies who suffer a cradle hell of insatiable cravings. Then we're familiar with another woman who's recognized internationally because of the nurture she extends to those who have been reduced to a childlike state through poverty or illness— Mother Teresa. The world calls these women "Mother" with a capital M.

I'm also aware of many other women who haven't received much press attention but who have picked up where biological mothers have left off. If I were an artist, these are the pairs I would try to capture on my canvas, mother and child—mother and someone else's child.

A friend told me about a young woman who recently had a baby. Estranged from her own parents, this inexperienced mom had no one to talk to about breast feeding, childhood diseases, or the fears that accompany being a new mother. An older woman in the church decided to adopt this new mom and her young family. Together they calmed newborn crying. Together they laughed at things that might have frightened a young mother forced to face them alone. The older woman passed on to the younger the old skills of caring for a baby. Together they welcomed a new babe into the world.

Here's another picture I would paint for the world to remember. A pastor's wife told me about a woman in their congregation. While watching the evening news she was moved by the story of a young boy. Distraught over an impending divorce, the boy's father had gone to the bedroom of his two young sons, and while they were sleeping, he shot them both and then committed suicide. The older boy, an eight-year-old, survived—with massive head wounds.

This Christian woman called the hospital to find out about his condition and discovered that he had been abandoned by his mother and grandparents. Everyone had given up hope for his recovery; he had been strapped in bed to restrain him; they had left him to do his dying alone.

She arranged to go and sit with him. Sharing twelve-hour shifts with her husband, she held this little boy, sang to him, prayed for him, loved him. They dedicated their lives to him during that critical time until the boy, whom no one dared to hope for, survived. Although they had no legal relationship with him when the caring process began, he now lives with them, and though he is disabled, he seems to be doing well in every other way.

Here's another portrait that stands out in today's world. A woman in Arizona gives comfort care to babies who are wards of the state. In her own home she cares for anencephalic babies—babies born without brains, but with brainstems that keep their functions automatic—to ease their dying process. There are usually several babies at a time in her home, requiring her to hire help in her care-giving mission. The short, tragic lives of these babes are infused with meaning and dignity by this woman's nurture. Why does she do it? Because she cares, because she practices the art of taking care of babies, because she's mastered the necessary skills.

Here's another beautiful scene, one that's filled with children's faces. A young mother cares for a foster child and then, with great effort, tracks down the other eight brothers and sisters and brings them all together to be raised in her home. It means buying a larger home, convincing state authorities that one woman is up to the task, but one by one she removes the obstacles so these children can be raised as brothers and sisters. This is a woman who still believes in the values of family and has dedicated her life to mastering its techniques.

I'm moved by these stories, but I sense they are the exceptions rather than the rule. These men and women are mothers and fathers with capital M's and F's, living with us, on our blocks, next door, in our own homes. You probably know one. You may even be one.

These are the parents I would capture in my painting. I would paint the too-old-to-have-children-at-home hand, wrinkled, giving care to the newborn. I would mix the colors in my palette to contrast the hues of their skin color. Dark and light blended in a relationship of care. To be gifted in nurturing is a blessing that carries a responsibility. The painting on my canvas would be of those who have lifted their eyes and extended their hearts beyond their own four walls to the needs of a hurting world.

Do you have a way with babies? Can you make a toddler forget a tantrum and laugh instead? Have you developed a shampooing technique that avoids the tears? Can you make peanut butter and jelly sandwiches seem like a feast? Do you know the right words to say when a child is afraid or depressed? If so, then you are an excellent caregiver—a nurturer with developed skill. You are potentially a mother with a capital M or a father with a capital F.

If you have the gift of nurturing, please don't withhold your giftedness from this world. It would be a tragic mistake to put your skills on a shelf simply because your own children are grown or because you are not married. It would be a great error not to practice your gift because of its current place of low esteem in our societal value system. Or if you're still raising a family, don't fall into the mistake of being so "family centered" that you hoard your care only for your own fortunate family. Caring for children is an extremely valuable skill that is scarce these days. It may be the most significant gift you could choose to spend your life giving.

Are you unable to give birth to children, longing for a child of your own? Don't grieve for long. Your longing to love a child need not go unexpressed. Look around you. Someone needs that love you so desperately want to give.

Are your children gone, emptying your nest and heart in the process? Then look around. Many little ones need a nest where they can receive what you are so good at giving.

Are you far from your loved ones? Then don't hoard that love for occasional holiday celebrations. Love is too valuable an asset to be tucked away in waiting. Give it to someone who will thrive on your nurturing care.

What I'm saying is suggested in the blessing from Isaiah 54:1–2, 13:

> "Sing, O barren woman, you who never bore a child
> [Sing, empty-nested woman, whose children are gone.
> Sing, nurturer, whose heart goes out to someone else's
> child.]; burst into song, shout for joy, because more are
> the children of the desolate woman than of her who has
> a husband," says the Lord.

> "Enlarge the place of your tent, stretch your tent curtains wide, do not hold back. [Open your heart, enlarge your heart, don't withhold your skills, don't withhold your love]. . . .
>
> "All your sons will be taught by the LORD, and great will be your children's peace."

I fear that our generation can't make the assumptions that Elizabeth Barrett Browning made about the women of her time when she wrote:

> Women know
> The way to rear up children
> They know a simple, merry, tender knack
> Of tying sashes, fitting baby-shoes,
> And stringing pretty words that make no sense.

I sense our societal values are removing us further from those women and men who have practiced the art of nurturing. We may be becoming, as Harriet Beecher Stowe once wrote, less and less like "those remarkable women of olden times, [who] are like the ancient painted glass—the art of making them is lost; my mother was less than her mother, and I am less than my mother."

I would reappraise the value of nurturing men and women in our high-tech, achievement-oriented day. I would remind us that these developed skills, practiced so well in former days, may be in danger of being nearly forgotten in our own time.

If you're good with children, you have great value in today's culture. The Lord may have plans to make you a mother with a capital M—the mother of many children—some of whom may be children not of your womb. The Lord may want you to be the father of a large family, a family of someone else's kids. I applaud the skills of the nurturers among us. If you're a caregiver, I admire your art. I sing your praise today. I shout for joy at the beauty of your skills. May you enlarge your "tent" to include the children who need your love. May all your children (those of your womb and not of your womb) be taught by the Lord, and may your peace and the peace of your many children be great.

EIGHT

Come Play at Our House!

I do not believe in a man's Christianity if the children are never to be found playing around his door.

      George MacDonald

"What do I do about this situation?" I recently asked my mother-in-law, a woman whose wisdom I value. "One of the boys' friend's mom is divorced and has recently begun living with a man. I'm uncomfortable with our boys staying there overnight. I want to be sure Brendan and Justin know that we don't approve of the arrangement. But I also want them to know that we still care about this friend's family. When I talked to our boys about it, they were surprised that I thought the situation was wrong. It's hard for them to understand that a parent, who seems basically nice, would openly do something that was wrong. Did you ever face this kind of stuff when you were raising your kids, Mom?"

She thought for a minute and then answered, "Well, actually I don't think we ever did. Everyone was raising children with the same values back then. Truthfully, Valerie, that was a situation I never had to deal with."

We are living in times of unprecedented change. Shifting morals are changing the lives of people all around us, but I found a solution. It was to have more of the play and overnights at our house. We've had to say no to invitations for campouts and weekend trips when the sleeping arrangements of the adults were questionable. That's been painful for all of us, but as parents, we must be willing to take the responsibility for the values to which our kids are exposed.

Long ago I began to instruct my children to call home and get approval for any videos they watched in other people's homes. I learned the hard way. In first grade Justin watched an R-rated movie at a friend's house. And while I'm constantly amazed at what some parents think is permissible, I'm also aware that I stand out as a prude in a permissive parental society. My children have had to come home when the video viewing has been too violent or sexual at a friend's home. This is awkward for all of us, yet I notice my children often begin their conversation about it with these words, "Mom, you won't believe what they're watching there. I didn't want to stay."

Yes, we are living in times of unprecedented change. Technology is changing our habits, but I've found a solution. Now I take the initiative and welcome our children's friends to our house for videos of our choice. I provide plenty of snacks and a friendly atmosphere. It seems to be working out just fine.

Over the years the answer to many of our problems lay in having the children's friends in our home. It was during this time that I began to notice a major shift in my attitude. I was thinking more and more about our boys' friends. I began to realize that in many cases, not only were my children better off at our house, but so were a few of their friends. The thriving atmosphere I had worked so hard to establish in our home nourished not only the native variety of child but transplants as well.

"Mom, Jeff's mom is always screaming at Jeff. I feel sorry for him. She's mean to him."

"Come play at our house!"

"Mom, Ellen's sister is always picking on her. She hates her!"

"Come play at our house!"

"Mom, Jamie's dad has a stack of *Playboy* magazines in their family room."

"Come play at our house!"

I had always greeted my own children at the end of the day, usually at the back door. "Hi! B. [short for Brendan] Hi! Justie-boy!" Now I include any extra children in the greeting, using their names, or for regulars their acquired names. At the Bell house Scott is Scottie (accent on the last syllable), Annie is Annie-Anne, Molly is Miss Molly. My family has always used nicknames as a form of giving affection. Children understand the welcome behind their Bell-household nicknames. I suggest the children call me Wonderful Sweet Precious Mrs. Bell. This is a joke they enjoy using when there's something they really want from me.

First-time visitors to a meal at our home are treated to celebrity status with a game we learned from the David and Karen Mains' household. While we're eating, everyone is allowed to ask the visitor one question. The only rule is the questioner must answer honestly. We ask questions like, "If money were no option, where would you spend your dream vacation?" or "If you had a million dollars, what would you do?" or "If you were the president of the United States, what law would you create?" These help us become acquainted with our visitor and teach our children how to be conversant and interested in someone else.

Children who have eaten with us before are assigned chores of setting tables and clearing up afterward along with our boys. I am an equal opportunity hostess!

I treat these kids as if they were my own. I correct swearing with, "You're too great a kid to use that kind of language. Please stop." I try to break up arguments with, "If this doesn't stop right now, you'll all be assigned to separate rooms for the next ten minutes until you cool off." I assume the traditional maternal role for any child under my roof.

Snacks are on hand but are of the cheapest variety: bulk apples, frozen pops, cookies. Visiting children are welcome to help themselves, but no one—*no one*—eats in the living room. And woe to the child who leaves wrappers or apple cores lying around!

We try to be inclusive. The boys take turns inviting friends to go to ball games and church activities or out for pizza with our family. We say yes whenever possible, saving no for times when it's absolutely necessary.

I said no the other day. We were invited to a friend's house. The boys wanted to bring our neighbor Molly. Molly desperately wanted to come because it was a holiday from school, and without us she would go home to an empty house because her mom was working. She had called her mom for permission before she checked with me. She asked Brendan and Justin to persuade me to let her come. They applied the pressure. I was uncomfortable imposing Molly on my unsuspecting hostess. "No, it's just not going to work out this time." I was emphatic. "This is just a family invitation." And then without missing a beat, Brendan declared, "But Mom, Molly is family!"

My message, however, had gotten through to my sons. These boys—who have had to learn to share everything they own with other people's kids, who have had to wait in line to play with their own toys, who have had to work through their relationships with some challenging personalities because Mom wouldn't send the other child away—understood. There are my co-laborers in an effort of caring. They participate in this mission unreservedly. I'm proud of their willingness to share the label "family" with other children who need it.

In the attempt to include as many children as possible, we've hosted some strange parties. When the children were small, we had a Cabbage Patch doll party. Invitations were printed out on the computer, dolls were dressed in their party best, and we had miniature refreshments (peanut butter and jelly sandwiches cut into shapes with cookie cutters). A cartoon video was rented from the store and dolls were put into a laundry basket to view the show from their front-row, box seats.

As the boys grew, our parties changed. We used to host a "capture the flag" party every summer. Kids are invited from all parts of the city. Admission is free, but everyone is encouraged to bring a group snack—popcorn, cookies, red licorice strings. We provide the drinks. We tell the children to wear dark clothes (for maximum night-time camouflage) and to have their parents pick them up at 9:30. Sometimes we've had thirty to forty children sneaking through our backyards looking for flags and hostages.

Our neighborhood children have also organized a summer Olympics. The children work for days, constructing medals and ribbons. Dads get together "the morning of" and construct obstacle courses, balance beams, bike-racing courses. Some of the entries are just a little different—break dancers, dog trainers, joke tellers. Awards night may coincide with a block party so the whole neighborhood can participate. It's an idea children love and could easily be adapted to most neighborhood settings.

Why not save dish-detergent squirt bottles and let the kids in your neighborhood have a water fight with their "weapons of choice"? It would be even better if parents got involved! The idea isn't just to have a party but to organize things that say we delight in children. We enjoy having them around.

"Come play at our house!" will look different in every home. One friend of mine keeps a box of toys that her own children have outgrown to entertain younger neighbor kids when they visit.

Another friend keeps a take-it-with-you box in their back closet. The box has old jewelry, hats, books, discarded toys. There children can sift for treasures to take home with them when they leave.

I even know a pastor who keeps a drawer full of matchbox cars in his office so visiting children can occupy themselves when their parents drop in for a chat. That says something about his level of comfort with children, doesn't it? It indicates that children aren't to be shoved off into a corner somewhere while adults conduct their business. Come play in my office! I like that!

One woman described the way welcome was extended to her as a little girl growing up: "I remember two elderly women from my own childhood in the 1930s. My friend, Helen, and I were typical tomboys—wild, rambunctious, and clumsy; but something happened to us when we dressed up in our mother's dresses, hats, and high heels to visit Miss Ramsey and Mrs. Shaw in their 'fussy' house on the corner of Fifth and Plum.

"We would be invited in with, 'We're so glad to see you, Miss Elliot and Miss Smith. How charming you look today!' We would click-clack to 'our' drawer for paper-doll books, crayons, and scissors.

"Conversation would follow. Our problems, our joys were listened to with interest. We were treated like *real* people. We were important enough to be served tea and cookies, and not at the kitchen table, but from a beautifully set table in the dining room!"

All I can say is, not only is that a lovely example of welcome extended to someone else's child, but it obviously made an unforgettable impression for my friend to write about it so fondly fifty years later.

Are we creating for some child memories that will become more precious when the child grows and remembers us? One woman shared this with me: "Every day I pray for the ghetto and underprivileged children. I remember the kind woman who gave my brother and me hot tea with sugar and bread and butter at lunch time when we were so poor we didn't have a school lunch. I remember the smell and taste of the tea and the warmth of her kitchen." Christian families who say, "Come play at our house!" may be making the best childhood memories some kids will ever have.

Sense the love and pride in this woman's memories about her mother: "I cry when I remember how my mother cared for a certain 'Molly' in our neighborhood. My mom used to bring her home and bathe her. She was such a dirty girl without much love . . . until, in came *my mom!*"

The year Brendan turned thirteen he chose to have a birthday party at home instead of roller skating or bowling. I thought it might be boring for his guests—perhaps just a little too old-fashioned—playing games at home with our family. About halfway through the party I noticed a friend of his sitting alone on the couch. I sat down and asked him what he was thinking about. He said he was thinking that his mom would flip if kids were making such a mess in her house. "She would probably throw down a tarp all over the carpet and Scotch-guard all the furniture before she would let all us kids in. She would never let me have a party like this!" His words were meant to be humorous, but there was a longing in them as well.

We are living in times of unprecedented change. Many of the changes have adversely affected children. Like Brendan's friend, many children may long for homes that are more accepting, more interested in them, more involved. For some it is an elusive dream.

Christian families can make better childhood memories for some of these children. We need to learn to say, "Come play at our house!" We need to say it often, and we need to say it sincerely.

NINE

Spiritual Dreamers, Holy Schemers

Some men see things as they are and say, why?
I dream things that never were and say, why
not?

George Bernard Shaw

I'm always encouraged when I find that others share my concern about children. But I'm thrilled when I meet other men and women who not only share my concern but also are taking a similar journey in learning to love someone else's child. With a certain relief we share our stories with each other. We are at different stages in our understanding of what is happening to us. Sometimes we still hear some reluctance in our voices. But every story is important because it indicates how God's Spirit is directing the lives of his people.

I believe that loving other people's children is actually an old, old story. The ancient biblical account tells of Pharaoh's daughter finding the Hebrew baby, Moses, in the bulrushes and taking him to her heart as her own child. God used this action not only to save one Hebrew baby but also to set an entire nation free from slavery. I perceive an element of redemption in all these stories—old or new—as God softens adult hearts to begin caring for a child who is not their own. When one child is cared for, an entire nation may feel the effect.

Though this work of caring for children is already in process, it deserves attention and encouragement to foster its growth. The following stories may inspire you to become involved or may encourage you if you are already involved.

"We have several children of our own, and so there are a lot of children in our home all the time," one woman recently wrote. "Several children stand out. One was Meredith—a real bully. She was the daily intrusion you described, but we always tried to include her in our family activities—from larger family birthday parties, trips to the zoo, even a vacation in Disney World. My justification was so she could see a different way of life than her birth environment. It just seemed her older parents no longer had the will or energy to do for her anymore. There were many confrontations, misunderstandings—but we persisted with Christian patience.

"There is so much pain and anxiety in this work. One of the biggest challenges is from well-meaning friends who believe [gaining] peace and tranquillity is our purpose on earth and that these children have no place in that goal."

Another woman writes, "I am awed at the 'unattended' children in our neighborhood. The other day a three-year-old was playing in our yard. The mother drove off without saying a word to me. I watched the child, but I could have had an appointment or an errand to run.

"There are children who play in the park near us. I'm talking about eight-, nine-, and ten-year-olds smoking, drinking, using foul language, and fighting. I myself broke up a fight the other day as a teenager kept hitting a younger girl. The younger walked away, but the older girl followed.

It seems the job of parenting goes to anyone who will 'watch.'"

Several stories from older people contrast with the we've-served-our-time attitude of some in the older generation. This is how one older woman describes "Come play at our house!":

"My husband turned seventy-eight recently, and I am seventy-six. We still enjoy little friends at our house. We ask parents if their little ones would like to spend some time at our house. We have toy boxes still, but the rule is the toys must be picked up before the children leave. We enjoy these children very much."

Another older woman writes, "I am a seventy-two-year-old widow living on social security. Two years ago a family moved in next door with a seven-year-old girl—Betsy. She weighs more than she should; she's nine now and wears a size sixteen.

"For some reason she keeps coming over any time. If I'm taking a nap, she keeps ringing the doorbell until she wakes me up. She says she comes for peace and quiet because her mom and dad do a lot of arguing. She says she wishes they were divorced.

"Some days she spends two to three hours with me, playing all kinds of games. I play the piano, and she loves to sing, so I've taught her several songs like, 'Let the Sunshine In,' 'Do Lord,' 'Jesus Loves Me,' 'I Have Decided to Follow Jesus,' and others.

"I wonder how many little Betsys are in this world. Betsy's parents won't let her go to church with me. But I guess I'm the only friend she has.

"Sometimes when I'm tired, I almost wish she would leave me alone, but this would not be a very good witness. So I love her for Jesus' sake. Who knows how these hours will affect her life in the future?"

Here's another good story: "When I was newly married, I had two little seven-year-old girls who came into my life. They would hang around when I worked outside. They both came from divorced homes. Neither mother gave them too much time.

"I took them in and grew to love them very much. We had pizza parties, went on shopping trips, and occasionally they would spend weekends with us. Even my husband grew to love them.

"They were around to help when my own children were born. Whenever they had problems, they would come and talk to me. They called me 'Secret Keeper.'

"I watched them grow up and get married. Now each has her own firstborn. I pray for their families to come to the Lord."

"I had a 'Jason' in my life," one woman writes. "His name was Ben, and his needs were great. When I first met him, he was an undisciplined, dirty, mean four-year-old. We met while I was walking our dog, and before long he was a frequent visitor to our home. He acted as if he lived there and did everything in his power to stay in my favor.

"He would ask if he could spend the night, and so he'd stay over and go to church with us on Sunday. He really blossomed. He enjoyed the attention of my husband, since he had no father living with him. It was a special treat to have someone to 'wrassle' with.

"Ben's mother decided she couldn't keep him. She tried to get his father to take him, but Ben reported, 'He didn't want me.'

"'Why don't I live with you?' he suggested. 'I could sleep on the sofa. I don't take up much room.' It broke my heart.

"Shortly afterward Ben's mother decided to keep him but was evicted from her home. I had to say good-bye to Ben, knowing I would probably never see him again. I have had to put Ben in God's care and trust that he is okay and that his needs are being met. We are now applying to become foster parents. It was our experience with Ben that taught us about the capacity to love other people's children."

Here's a story that has been a while in its telling: "We used to have a neighbor who would clean her house and lock her children outside. It all started with the nine-year-old boy. He had to go to the bathroom, and his mom would not answer the door, so he came to me, and I let him in. I asked him to stay and played games with him and talked to him.

"Soon his sister started to come. The boy would come to Good News Clubs, but he always would disrupt them.

"Our family moved from that town, but on a visit back several years later, I ran into the mother in a fast-food restaurant. She said, 'Guess what happened after you moved?' She told me that both children and she and her husband had accepted the Lord. Also the girl had been married, and her husband was a believer. It is amazing how God can use us if we let him!"

"We have a variety of children in our neighborhood," another woman begins. "There were two children who, once I decided to open my yard to them, consistently spent the weekday afternoons in my yard. Sometimes I was totally disinterested in being with them, and yet I know God desires his servants to sacrifice their wants for his.

"One child was particularly obnoxious, but as I grew to know him, it seemed much [of his problem] came from the desire for attention and care. I didn't have to look further than my back door to find children who needed me.

"Most always I blunder through life just trying to survive day to day and find little time or energy to minister, which is to my disgrace. But I've been glad to be there for those kids.

"I also wanted to mention that I too had an older godly woman who took me under her wing when I was younger."

I enjoy hearing stories from men. "Little Joshua is an unusual six-year-old child and very lonely. My first encounter with him was in the front yard. He plays with children down the street, but many times they send him home.

"Talking with him one day he told me that 'they' were getting a divorce. Joshua said that his daddy is mean. My first reaction was, how can I show love to this child?

"He asked my name, and I told him 'Stephen.' Almost every day I hear a voice somewhere in the distance yelling, 'Hi, Stephen!' Joshua will have to do kindergarten over next year because of social problems, not because he's slow in any way. I have let him help me wash the car. He said, 'I think this is great that you let me help because I have never done this before.' I wouldn't have missed this for anything!"

"I met a little nine-year-old boy a while ago," another man says. "He fit in perfectly with my own kids, and soon he was spending the whole summer at our house. Needless to say, he gave us more than we gave him.

"Recently his family moved from our town. [Before they left,] his mother told me his stepfather wouldn't let him get close except to correct him. She was glad I had been able to show her son some male love. I feel as if I lost a child of my own!"

"I had an embarrassing experience the other day," a young mother writes. "Someone asked me how many children I have. I honestly could not remember how many I actually bore because along with my three, I baby-sit for three, and by the time you add my children's friends and assorted neighbor kids, I can easily have twelve children at my house on any given day. I've even had totally strange kids at my door begging to come in and just be there! It's a sad day for our country when you can hear the silent cry for 'Mommy.'"

Another letter begins, "Because of hearing you talk about loving other people's children, when a certain young neighbor girl kept showing up at my door asking to stay for supper, I was able to find room at our table and room in my heart for one more child. As a result of this, last night this same little girl had supper with us and accepted the Lord. I am so glad I took the gospel of Jesus Christ down off the shelf and put it out where others could find it!"

Some of the stories in my collection indicate a certain degree of awareness and organization. They are the stories of what one person can do, if that person can conceive a dream and convince others to help make it reality.

A grandmother writes, "I know of one Texas church, which is located near a public elementary school, that is open after school for children whose parents work—all children—not just the church's own members. The children can do crafts, do homework, or play basketball.

"My nine-year-old great grandson goes there after school as his parents work. There's only a small charge to cover snacks. I think this is a great setup!"

I do too! Here's another great idea: "The story is old; the solution is new. Marty, ten, needs help. After his mother and father divorced, Marty's life fell apart. He's often unsupervised for hours. Junk food is his regular diet; television, his best friend.

"Marty and his mother often fight. Marty usually wins. Marty even lived for a while with his grandmother. She was unable to handle him.

"Marty and thousands of children like him across our country need help! They need a family.

"A new solution: offer the 'Martys' of our nation a new start in a new family—a 'Greenhome' family.

"*Greenhomes America* is an organization that began in August 1987. It serves as a coordinating center for the networking of Christian foster homes. They provide the tools, the legal work, and counseling for families and congregations that will together take on the responsibility for these children who so often fall through the societal cracks. The local church provides the spiritual and financial support to the 'Greenhome' family. It's an opportunity for ministry for the whole congregation. I think it's an exciting new way to reach out to someone else's child."[1]

The stories of sidewalk Sunday schools, where the church goes to apartment complexes on weekdays and holds Sunday school and after-school clubs specifically for self-care children, are encouraging and need to be multiplied in communities all across this land.

I take a great deal of comfort from these stories. It is reassuring to know that there is an authenticity to the idea of caring for other people's children. There's something about it that rings true.

I imagine that some critics will dismiss the scheme of reaching out to other people's children as too idealistic to scratch the surface of children's problems. Skeptical voices will speak out prophesying doom. Others will shrug it all off in the apathetic and mistaken belief that our government will somehow be able to address children's problems without the private sector's help.

But despite the cynics, the critics, and the apathetic, some people will say, "Why not?" I anticipate that my collection will grow with wonderful, holy stories. Sometimes they will make us laugh, and sometimes they will break our hearts. When we read these stories, we will be reaffirmed in our direction. We will understand that we are participants in a movement that God may use for the redemption of a generation of lost American children. We journey with others who are spiritual dreamers and holy schemers. We travel in the best of company.

TEN

My God, My Neighbors, My Isaacs

Thus does the world forget Thee, its creator,
and falls in love with what Thou hast created
instead of with Thee.

Augustine of Hippo

Just a little exposure to other people's children evokes many questions. This is how one man described his problem: "My wife has been baby-sitting for a boy, Sammy, for two years. Sammy's mother has been in and out of alcohol, drugs, and men. As you can imagine, Sammy has his own set of problems and is a continuing bad influence on our children. Just last week I was telling my wife, 'Our kids have their own junk to deal with, and we don't need another kid around who has such a bad effect on our kids. I want him out of the house if he doesn't straighten up.' Then I heard you talk."

Another woman wrote, "I am the mother of two small children. The thing that bothers me the most is the influence of the neighborhood children on my own. I want to help the neighbors' children, but I sometimes fear for my own. It's a scary situation."

These are questions that need addressing when we become involved with children from families who do not share our value systems. In times past, Americans generally shared common values and agreed on what behavior was acceptable for children. Today all that has changed. In some cases it's not just that moms and dads fail to correct their children's negative behavior; instead, some kids are being "home-schooled" in offensive, unacceptable conduct.

More and more kids are learning from their parents to pepper their speech with gross expletives, crude inferences, and swearing. Many children who are treated roughly at home are being taught to handle conflict through physical aggression. Unless someone teaches these children a better method, they will carry these patterns into adulthood. Someone needs to run interference in their lives, to show them better ways of speaking, of interacting with other people.

Many Christian parents fear that their own children will learn this kind of negative behavior by being exposed to it. Instead, I have found that our own children who are exposed to it very often become inoculated against it. Your children may become as turned off by it as you are.

Actually, I've discovered an advantage to having the bad behavior visiting in your own home. Your children will learn how to handle it by watching you. I believe my children are much wiser for some of the "characters" we've learned to cope with together over the years.

If you will take the time to teach all the children what's wrong with some videos, why you object to some television programs, why drugs are dangerous, why smoking isn't "cool," your children as well as the others will benefit. If you care deeply about the words that are used and the impression they give, consistently insisting on cleaner talk, not only will your kids be mature by the time they take their first steps into the adult world, but you will enjoy an immeasurable ministry in the life of the other children as well.

By taking this position, we assume the parental role that is being abdicated in so many children's lives. By taking this role we commit ourselves to "raising," not just "tolerating," other people's kids. This type of surrogate parenting assumes an active interest in the development of a child who may not be receiving that kind of help at home.

I find that Christian parents most commonly err on the side of "pollution" control. When we look at the world in which we're bringing up our children, it's tempting to be overly protective. But I strongly believe that the best help we can give our own children to grow strong is not by shielding them from the world but by showing them how to grow straight and compassionate in it.

If all we've wanted for our children is that they would grow straight, then we have not wanted enough for them. We must teach them to be caring and understanding, to hurt when others hurt, and to be willing to sacrifice themselves to address others' pain. Growing straight without learning to relate to and care for a needy, though crooked, world, results in a judgmental, hard-hearted, self-righteous adult. That is a dangerous and repugnant possibility. Our own children benefit when we model caring for their peers.

I must add an important word here, though: Christian parents must differentiate between fear that arises out of overly protective tendencies and fear that arises from dangerous situations. One friend recently shared with me a frightening experience their four-year-old daughter had. She had gone to a neighbor's home to play. While she was there, a nine-year-old boy had frightened her into playing sexual games. She came home in tears, with bite marks on her vagina.

This mother and I suspected that this nine-year-old had been sexually abused and was passing his learned behavior on to someone he could victimize. But we also agreed that the safety and well-being of her little girl was more important than continuing the relationship with the other child. Remember that the interior rage of other "little birds" could harm your own child.

A parent's primary responsibility in situations that appear physically dangerous must always be the protection of their own child. I am not talking about situations where children push and shove; this is so common in the child world. What I'm referring to is overt, consistent tendencies to abuse. In these situations parents must be extremely watchful and ready to run interference. Generally, though, we Christian parents need not be overly protective when it comes to our children and other kids.

We also will encounter another problem when we have other people's children around. It is our tendency to be possessive of the ones we love. Parents and children alike may find sharing each other with "outsiders" poses a real struggle.

I remember having such feelings as a young girl. My father was a compassionate man and particularly felt for the ten children who lived next door to us. We had a rope swing, a real status symbol for kids back then. It hung from a tree that sat on the edge of a gully. At the peak of the rope's swing, my stomach would tie in knots and the distant ground below seemed to belong to mere mortals, whom I pitied in my exhilarating flight.

We loved to get my dad to push us. He was incredibly fun. He enjoyed getting into the act by spinning us like tops, speeding us to our appointments with the pits of our stomachs, and then scaring us on our return flight with horrible monster faces and terrifying sounds.

I suspect all the neighbor children were just a little in love with my dad because of his style, but none loved him more than I. I loved him with first love, a kind of vulnerable adoration. I loved him possessively, immaturely.

One day I learned the danger of such love. My parents' home always operated under the rule of "company first." That meant ten little neighbor kids would receive their turns swinging before any Burton child. "Mr. Buhton! Mr. Buhton!" the "extras" would squeal. "Me next! I called thirds" or "I got fourths!" The commotion would usually attract a crowd, and my father would try to give everyone a turn.

On this particular afternoon I impatiently waited my turn for my dad and my swing. But when it was my turn, he looked at me and said, "Lovey Dove, I'm just too tired to give you your turn now. We'll do it some other time."

My reaction couldn't have been stronger if he had struck me or told me he didn't love me. There was only one explanation for this rejection: he loved the neighbor kids better than he loved me!

I was too proud to let him see that I was wounded, but I poured it out in my five-year diary. Three words—I HATE DADDY! After my passion had cooled and our relationship had been restored, I was ashamed of those words. It seemed the diary would automatically open there and those three words would accuse me and show me what a terrible child I was. I hid my diary. I prayed no one would ever read those three terrible words—especially my father.

I've recognized this struggle in my own children. It wasn't long after Molly started coming to our house that Brendan shared with me a dream he had one night. He dreamed it was his birthday, and I had given all his presents to Molly! It doesn't take a Daniel to interpret that dream, does it?

How easily our human loves endanger and enslave us! How quickly they can become passions of selfishness, possessiveness, and jealousy. I've explained to my children that I love Molly in ways different from how I love them. I love Molly with compassion. I love her with God's love. I've had to work at loving Molly. I explain that I love them naturally, that I have to work at not loving them too much; I have to resist holding them too closely and squeezing our relationship to death.

I suspect a bit of this possessive love in the relationship between a woman who recently wrote me about her husband. She ran into trouble with him when she tried to extend hospitality to other people's children: "There is a little boy in our neighborhood to whom I've been reaching out. His mother locks him out of their house sometimes, and he's so lonely. My heart just goes out to him. The problem is my husband. He doesn't think the boy should be at our house so much, especially when he comes home from work. He just doesn't want to be bothered. I can't make him understand how strongly I feel about this. He wants me to stop having the child in."

Possessive love is immature love. It always looks out for its turn, its territory, its relationships. It is a kind of bondage and makes a slave of the heart it controls. It desires to be the only love, the only one receiving presents, the only one given a turn at the swing. All others must wait in line, take thirds and fourths, to such an immature love. When we love immaturely, we often expect God to understand when we turn to him and say, "Sorry, there just isn't time for you today. You understand, don't you?"

All our loves must be subordinated to our love for God. Otherwise they may rise up and demand inordinate placement in our lives. Our tendencies to overprotect and overpossess are indications that our loves have not been subordinated to our love for God. When God commanded that we should have no other gods before him, he wasn't speaking simply of primitive people's idol gods of their own creation. He was speaking of our loves. "You shall have no other loves before me" is what he says to us. All our human loves must be tempered by our love for God and subjugated to that great primary love.

We don't love our children or our spouses less when we allow other people's children a place in our hearts. We will love family members well when our primary love is for our Lord. We will also allow other people's children space in our hearts only when our primary love is for the Lord. These loves find balance with each other when the love of God is first. Jesus spoke of that great love when he said that the greatest commandment was to love the Lord your God with all your heart, soul, and mind.

He followed with the second greatest commandment: "Love your neighbor as yourself." We might have liked it better if he had said to love our families as ourselves, but perhaps he realized the tendencies of such loves to become our focus, our god.

This is our daily challenge: to love God with a primary love and to love our neighbors as ourselves. Love of God and love of neighbors, when combined, adjust our tendency simply to grow straight. These two loves protect our familial loves from becoming ugly passions of possessiveness and jealousy. Love of both God and neighbor motivates us to be inclusive—to share our presents, our swings, our family members. We cannot learn these two great loves too early or too well.

Possessive or immature loves stand in great contrast to the "perfect" mature love I read about recently in a magazine article.[1] It was about children whom no one wants, children whom most mothers don't want around their own children or around themselves for that matter. The subject of the piece is a secret society of foster parents who care for babies with AIDS. It focuses on Helen, a forty-one-year-old black woman. She shared her feelings about the twenty-one-month-old AIDS-afflicted child on her lap. "All of us have a season. But we make the most of what we have today. Does it make sense to avoid loving someone now because you might lose him later on? Do you stop going to the beach because summer is going to end? No! You have to say, 'Let's do patty-cake, Let's sing. Let's kiss on each other a little while.' Let's do all those mushy things that prolong the child's life."

The AIDS baby, Denise, is just a stick figure. Two tubes run from her nostrils down the back of her neck to a portable oxygen tank. She wakes up three to six times a night, and most nights Helen takes her to the bed she shares with her husband.

Where do these secret foster parents find the strength to love so selflessly and so courageously? The clue was in the last paragraph of the article. We're again at Helen's house, but several weeks have passed since the initial interview. "Mushy things no longer suffice. The doctors have prescribed morphine for Denise's pain and Helen has begun to sing, 'Jesus loves me! This I know!' as she rocks the child. 'It's okay to go,' she whispers. 'These arms will hold you again.' Denise heeds Helen's sweet voice and dies."

The Bible says perfect love casts out fear. That is the kind of love this woman offers. Perfect love simply doesn't count the cost or know how to protect its own interests. It simply and fearlessly responds to human suffering as Christ would.

No one can guarantee Helen that her work with AIDS babies won't someday be personally costly. No one can guarantee you that if you expose your children to other people's kids that your kids won't be influenced negatively. I can't

.promise you that your children or spouse will not feel displaced by an "extra" child or two. I can tell you that my son no longer worries about being displaced by someone else's child. If anything, Brendan is Molly's champion. I can also tell you that what caused me pain in my childhood has become one of my fondest childhood memories. It's with tenderness, not hatred, that I remember how my father included everyone's children in swinging until the point of exhaustion. What a guy!

I've learned that my heavenly Father can be quite unconventional when he wants to get something done. We may find God testing his place in our affections by asking us to sacrifice our Isaacs. With a concerned parental heart we, like Abraham, may worry about the strange work God is requiring of us, knowing that to do his will may affect our families. But we also need to have Abraham's faith that God will provide for "our own" when the story is finished. He is trustworthy. If he calls us to a work that requires faith, he will not abandon us to ourselves down the road. Instead, it is often the path of faith in which we receive our greatest spiritual blessings. "O taste and see that the LORD is good: blessed is the man that trusteth in him" (Ps. 34:8 KJV).

People in political office have been calling for the private sector to come forward and help address our societal needs. In his 1988 presidential campaign, former president George Bush used a picturesque phrase to capture the idea of thousands of individual Americans addressing our country's problems. "A thousand points of light," he called it.

But the man or woman of faith knows that when these lights are examined closely, many are altar fires, altars that burn with the sacrifices of ordinary people who have extraordinarily and willingly laid down their turns at the swing, their normal family life, their Isaacs, their personal conveniences, or future health to address the enormous needs of their "neighbors."

When God wants to address a problem in a nation, he very often calls forth Abrahams, people of faith, to do the unusual. Without a deep spiritual commitment to love of God and love of neighbor, the thousand points of light will quickly burn out—smothered by the inconvenience and bother of it all. Humanitarianism alone will not fuel the fires of self-sacrifice for long.

Only our love for God will keep the sacrificial fires burning. While the fires burn, those who love him must trust him to provide for their own Isaacs. "Love the Lord your God with all your heart and with all your soul and with all your mind" is the greatest commandment (Matt. 22:37). It is that love that helps us follow what may well be the hardest commandment, "Love your neighbor as yourself" (Matt. 22:39). It is perfect love.

ELEVEN

Characteristics of a Nurturing Person

Nurturance: affectionate care and attention.

> *Webster's New Collegiate Dictionary*

What does a nurturing person look like? This question is important for two reasons. First, we can all work toward becoming more nurturing in our relationships, and knowing what a nurturing person looks like helps us shape our goals. Second, parents who must leave their children with a caregiver need to know what qualities to look for in the adult they choose.

1. *Nurturers are compassionate people.* Someone has described compassion as "having your pain in my heart." That certainly describes an important characteristic of a nurturer. A nurturer has the capacity to feel another's pain. Nurturers feel for the working poor and single parents who must leave their children to provide for them. They are sympathetic, not judgmental. They are disturbed by the societal trends that victimize children—divorce, single-parent homes, increased poverty, and the like. Nurterers are moved to

address those problems personally. Put simply, a nurturer has the capacity both to care and to demonstrate that care.

2. *Nurturers maintain a sense of humor.* Nurturers are easily charmed by children since they hold the belief that children are innately funny. Nurturers set the emotional tone on a high, joyful level. They establish the emotional atmosphere themselves, rather than allow children to determine it. They *enjoy* children.

3. *Nurturers are even-tempered.* Nurturers will handle a crisis without making it a catastrophe. They don't overreact, causing the situation to become worse than it already is. They do not scream, yell, or have adult temper tantrums. They don't take their bad moods out on the people around them. They do not discipline other people's children physically. They are characterized by self-control in their behavior and in the things they say.

4. *Nurturers understand children.* Nurturers know the difference between misbehavior and developmental stages. Nurturers know how two-year-olds behave and are not undone when they behave like "terrible two-year-olds." They do not discipline or dislike children for acting their age. Nurturers know many ways to mold a child to correct behavior. Because nurturers know what to expect and how to stay a step ahead of the child, they can anticipate behavior and divert it before it gets out of hand.

As an elementary-school music teacher I had the opportunity to deal with many different age groups. I'll never forget one experience, however; it pointed out how much more I needed to learn about first graders. I was writing on the chalkboard, with my back turned to the class, a very dangerous thing to do at the beginning of the school year, when first graders behave more like squirrels than human beings.

I glanced over my shoulder as I was writing and discovered that every child was crawling on the floor. "What in the world?" I started to say. "How dare you all get out of your seats while I'm teaching!" But before I could say anything, a child on the floor near me said, "Will you give us all stars now? We all did a good thing and picked up pieces of paper that were on the floor. Our classroom teacher gives us stars if we do good things without being told."

I hadn't understood how motivated first graders are to please and to achieve in any reward system or how susceptible they are to "group think." They weren't being disruptive, in their thinking at least. They were trying to please me and get rewarded besides. I didn't yell at them, but I didn't reward them either. I guess we all learned a lot about each other that day.

5. *Nurturers express affection.* Children enjoy being warmly greeted and slightly "fussed over." It is easy for nurturers to hug, pat, and warmly smile at children. Nurturers convey to children that they are special. "I like being with you" is the message they get across by words, attitudes, and significant touches.

6. *Nurturers are not competitive.* Nurturers may have children of their own, but they do not pit their children against others competitively. Beware of the parent whose child walked, talked, and was potty-trained before anyone else's and who let the whole world know it. Beware of the mother whose children are not taught to share, to take turns, or to speak politely to others.

Nurturers can enjoy the superior characteristics of other people's children without feeling their own child is inferior. They don't feel their child needs to be number one all the time, and they can therefore encourage other children in their areas of giftedness. Nurturers believe there's room for all types in the world and therefore are not threatened by other children's achievements.

7. *Nurturers practice an open lifestyle*. Nurturers don't have dark secrets hidden from view. Nurturers can unashamedly open their homes to others without fear of something terrible being "discovered." "What you see is what you get" is how they live, and they aren't ashamed by anything others would discover about them. They aren't necessarily perfect, but they don't feel they have to hide anything either.

This is the opposite of many adults who are hiding alcoholism, drug abuse, physical or sexual abuse, homosexuality, and a myriad of addictions and psychological problems, hoping no one will discover these dark personal secrets. Psychologists are discovering that one characteristic of dysfunctional families is that they keep dark family secrets. The keeping of secrets leads to unhealthy emotional makeup and disqualifies some who would be potential caregivers.

8. *Nurturers maintain a sense of wonder and awe toward life*. They display a sense of discovery and enjoy exposing children to the world. Nurturers don't use the television as a baby-sitter but instead are actively involved in all activities.

9. *Nurturers are trustworthy*. Nurturers are there when they're needed. They don't gossip about other people's children. They wouldn't destroy even a child's reputation.

10. *Nurturers value life and believe in God*. Nurturers understand that they cooperate in a holy venture when they reach out to a hurting child. They have a sense of mission in their dealings with children. Their lives point toward God both in the things they say and in the way they live. Theirs is a gentle work, more caught than taught, but it is an increasingly important work in a society that grows more secular all the time. Nurturers believe they are strategically placed by God and minister his love unreservedly to those with whom they come into contact.

11. *Nurturers can see the inner child whom others miss.* Nurturing people reach out to all ages, knowing that many hurting adults harbor an inner child who keeps crying for love. Nurturers can look past the age of the skin to the hurt inner child whose needs have gone unaddressed and unsatisfied for too many years.

As you read the list, I'm sure you would agree that this world could certainly benefit if there were more real nurturers around. Or perhaps you feel discouraged, realizing that a nurturer is close to a saint and that to become one will require a real stretch of your abilities. Or perhaps you have a baby for whom you're trying to find a good caregiver, and you're discouraged that no one you know matches the list.

Don't be discouraged. God intends to do a good work among us. I believe that few things would please the Lord more than to equip his people to meet the needs of the lonely children around us.

Nurturing is an acquired skill. It can be learned. I believe that God can soften hearts, then teach those softened hearts the work they need to do. I believe that God is in control, not only over the nations, but also over our individual lives. We matter to him. Children matter to him.

I love those Scripture verses that indicate the care God demonstrates toward children. "See that you do not look down on one of these little ones. For I tell you that their angels in heaven always see the face of my Father in heaven" (Matt. 18:10).

A system is already in place to provide for the needs of "these little ones." I'm encouraged simply to be part of a puzzle, a divine plan, to help meet the needs of some nearby child. We don't work alone. We work in cooperation with God and his angelic hosts to bring about a work for good in the lives of those for whom he so greatly cares.

TWELVE

Little Girls! Little Boys!

There was an old woman who lived in a shoe.
She had so many children she didn't know
what to do.

Nursery Rhyme

It was Illinois's hottest summer in fifty years. For a record number of days the mercury unmercifully topped the 100-degree mark. It was hard to find relief from the oppressive heat. Because the heat was accompanied by drought conditions, our town placed a ban on water usage. The neighborhood children couldn't even enjoy the traditional summer relief of running through lawn sprinklers.

For weeks we had been living in our basement, like a family of ground-dwelling rodents. It was the coolest place in our old prairie-style house. We were all uncomfortable and irritable. How I hated to go upstairs to the kitchen to try to fix meals! I went to great lengths to avoid turning on the stove and increasing the intense heat in the house. My solution was to fix salads for evening meals—taco salads, chicken salads, tuna salads, spinach and bacon bit salads. Anything to keep the heat down in the house.

And so it was that my "friend" Molly nearly forfeited her childhood in my kitchen one summer morning. I had left the house in the morning for an hour's work at my office.

When I returned, Molly was already at our house. As I walked through the back door into the kitchen, I was greeted with an incredible blast of heat and the distinct smell of chocolate chip cookies.

"Hi, Valerie!" she chirped. "I thought I would make your family some chocolate chip cookies. I would have made them at my house, but Mom doesn't let me bake in the kitchen when she's not home."

Now remember, Molly is one resourceful little girl. She knows when I'm at work. She also knows that baking in her kitchen on an already hot summer day will make her house unbearable. Immediately I suspected this was Molly's version of having her cake and eating it too. No doubt Molly intended to take most of those cookies and eat them in the privacy of her "cooler" home where there was no mother present to nag her about her diet.

How should I handle this? I wondered, as my boiling point rose, threatening to surpass the temperature in my kitchen. I could . . .

Option 1—Seize the teachable moment and use it as an object lesson about hell. I might say something like, "Imagine living in this kind of heat for eternity. And we thought Illinois summers were something!"

Option 2—Scream. Throw a tantrum. Feed the cookies to the dog, then move away from the neighborhood!

Option 3—Be adult. Say as pleasantly as possible, "Molly, I don't want you cooking in my kitchen when I'm gone either. Next time check with me first."

I opted for the third choice, but the episode made something clear to me. It's not just your own children who occasionally drive you up a wall. Sometimes that "extra" child or "extra" children are just too much even for someone who cares deeply for them.

I have to laugh at the orphan-keeper's song from the musical *Annie*. If ever a woman needed a break from being with kids, it was Miss Hannigan. She had obviously had her fill of little girls. Many of us can identify with her frustrations:

> Little girls, little girls,
> everywhere I turn—I can see them.
> Little girls, little girls,
> night and day I eat, sleep, and breathe them!

Miss Hannigan didn't mention little boys, but when we speak of the stress of constantly dealing with children, wouldn't it be unfair to overlook the male version of Miss Hannigan's lament?

> Little boys, little boys,
> roughhousing around my best dishes.
> Little boys, little boys,
> suddenly, it's tears and stitches!

Those silly little verses speak some truth. How many times have I been talking with another mother, only to suddenly realize (with some consternation) that a miniature set of feminine ears is straining to hear our every word? Have you ever noticed how little girls love to hang around when "adult" conversation is taking place?

And if little boys don't usually get on adult nerves in that way, they have their own annoying tendencies. You can forget having a decent conversation when little boys decide to pump up the volume of their play.

So if "annoyed" occasionally describes how you feel about the little girls and boys in your life, if the kids in your neighborhood are beginning to make you feel like screaming, then you may need a break from your routine. Don't feel guilty. You don't have an unusual reaction to children. You're not a nasty adult. You are normal and experiencing typical adult reactions from being overexposed to the child world. Your nervous system may realize that you need some space before your brain registers the fact. Needing privacy doesn't mean you're a self-centered person. Young mothers especially need privacy to restore their ability to interact with the child world. Without a certain amount of space, adults can easily overdose on children and then experience guilt about the resentment and anger they feel.

Under certain circumstances even the most loving and tolerant adult can feel that there are too many children in the house, too much of the time.

A young mother shared her situation with me. "I am a reluctant Kool-Aid Mom. I like my privacy. Sometimes I resent stepping into my backyard and finding it full of children. I'd like to take my baby outside to push him in the swing without all the little neighborhood girls flocking around arguing over whose turn it is to push him. I'd like to pitch balls to my two sons without having the whole neighborhood line up for turns. Sometimes I feel as if I have to go to a park in order to spend time with my own children—and yet I sense God's call. I sense the importance of our place in the neighborhood. I baby-sit for three other children during the day."

When I read that letter, I thought I had the writer pegged until I read the last line—"I baby-sit for three other children during the day." Then I knew what she was trying to say. Too many kids, too much of the time.

Burnout is a term often used in professional circles to describe what happens to people who are overexposed and overworked in their professional lives. It also describes perfectly what happens to many women who spend time with children every day. Children can just be too day-in-day-out constant.

We all need a certain amount of privacy. Unfortunately privacy is harder to find around lots of children. I read about one mother who would throw her apron up over her head when she had had enough. Her kids knew it was "the sign" to give their mom some space.

I can endure and enjoy much more interaction with children than I would sometimes like to admit, but when I begin to feel things are intolerable, I have to give the kids a sign that I need some space. The young mother who wrote me is in that situation. Baby-sitting, taking care of her own children, serving as the neighborhood Kool-Aid Mom—all this constant involvement with children may easily cause her to overdose in her role of nurturer. But how can she get that needed break?

We need to give children signs that don't humiliate or reject them but clearly set the limits we need. These verbal cues may help you tell your children that you've had enough.

"The yard is open for another half hour and then everyone will have to find another place to play for the day."

"Sorry, my children can't play today. But they would love to play tomorrow."

"The family room is off-limits to kids today. I'm in here now. But you can play in the bedrooms if you can play quietly."

"Sorry, my children aren't here now. You can come back and play with their toys when they're home."

It's important to know when your nervous system is saying "enough already!" It's also important to your relationship with these children that you don't allow yourself to become hostile or aloof without explaining why.

Because availability is important to many children who have no other adult they can approach, don't use these words simply for the sake of convenience or as a matter of general policy. Use them sparingly, when you feel that without some space, you'll burst!

Discover the things that restore you, perk you up, make you feel better about yourself and the world around you. Plan those things into your day as a part of your routine to take care of yourself. And try some of these burnout busters.

1. *Change your routine.* Make every day unique in some way. Nothing can inspire you less than the same old grind. Put on some tapes and sing along, or do aerobics with some available preschooler. That's always good to get the laughter back in your life.

2. *Get out of the house,* but don't just go to the mall. It's too easy to get into the habit of trying to restore yourself by buying new things all the time. Go someplace where you can look at beautiful things (nature, art), read stimulating books (the library), or enjoy people you like. A cup of coffee at a friend's house can be a great boost for both of you.

3. *Laugh at yourself.* Realize that sometimes we overreact to situations that really aren't all that bad. So Molly made the kitchen an inferno. The house is still standing; it could have been worse!

4. *Have a quiet place.* I *hate* to send children home, even when I'm in the worst of moods. So I have a "private spot" I can go to when I'm feeling overwhelmed. It's my area where I can read, nap, or write. The children know that I don't want to be disturbed when I'm there. If they want me, they need to knock on the door before coming in. Some of the children understand this so well that they will answer the doorbells and phones for me when I'm busy in my "private spot." I don't need to ask; they just know I appreciate it, and they do it for me.

5. *Learn to say no.* Sometimes you will run into people who, sensing your generous spirit, will try to take advantage of

you. A friend told me of one child's mother who would call them at the beginning of every month (before they could possibly have other plans) and try to tie up their weekends taking care of her child. Learn to protect yourself by saying no when enough is enough. In the case of my friend, saying no meant long sessions explaining why, phone calls pleading for her to change her mind, and attempts to make her feel guilty. Hold your ground, and keep saying no until everyone gets the message that you mean it.

Being a Kool-Aid Mom doesn't mean that you let everyone walk all over you. It doesn't mean that you look out for everyone except yourself. It is a position of ministry and dignity. You are doing an important work when you become involved with other people's children, but don't minimize your own needs in the process.

Maintaining some control over our privacy will mean we're much less prone to be reluctant Kool-Aid Moms. We shouldn't underestimate the importance of restoration. If you deserve a break, find a way to take it, and then take it without guilt.

THIRTEEN

Who Cares About the Working Mom?

"This mother was no great thing," added the Thenardiess. "She abandoned her child."

Victor Hugo
Les Misérables

The other day in the doctor's waiting room I witnessed a working mom's nightmare. A young mother was seated holding an adorable baby girl, dressed in frills, ready to see the doctor. The mother cooed over her, smiling down at her. I thought, *How nice that she enjoys her child!* Then in a flash, with a personality change that could rival the speed of Miss Piggy's, the mother started screaming in the direction of the play area where a pair of twins were playing. Two little sets of eyes topped by undone tousled hair looked up. "Get over here, sit down, and shut up!" she spat the words with a venomous staccato. The mother, who moments ago was dripping with sweetness, had become a shrew.

After the forlorn twins sat down (fighting for the seat farthest from the woman), I got the real picture. "Is that our car in the parking lot?" one little voice inquired. "That's not *our* car," the woman shot back. "That's *my* car!"

That's when I realized that the twins were not hers. This woman was taking care of another woman's children!

Not only did she hold the twins in contempt, but she totally disregarded the trust their mother had placed in her. I shuddered to think a mother would be reduced to leaving her children with such an inappropriate caregiver. I cringed to think what the caregiver might be like when she wasn't in a public place, where no one could see or hear her. What's worse than a caregiver who abuses the trust someone has put in her?

But who cares about working moms these days anyway? It's their job to look after their own children, right? The rest of us have our own problems.

Have you been in a situation like this before? You're in a Sunday school discussion group or women's Bible study, and the subject turns to working moms. Suddenly the discussion becomes very intense. Someone has made a generalization that *every* mom should stay home with her children. That statement is usually followed by another—"I did!" and the implied though unstated, "You should too!"

The "I dids" are rarely single mothers or widows but women married to someone who could provide enough for them to stay home even if they had to sacrifice and scrape to do so.

Some defensive voice will often pipe up, "Well, I wish I could stay home, but I can't."

So we come to our classic standoff, with the "I dids" and the "You should toos" on one side and the "I can'ts" on the other. Although the issue is far from resolved, one thing is certain. It's gotten hostile in there.

I've been in so many of these discussions in church settings that I'm beginning to wonder if God's people don't hold working moms in some disregard too. Who cares about the working mom today, anyway?

"Dear whoever was talking on the radio today," a letter I received recently began so personally. (That should have been my first clue, but I read on anyway.) "How I must talk to YOU today! (That should have been my second clue—when they start capitalizing you, what follows can be a real stinger!) It is not an accident that I've chosen this particular stationery today (pink with Mom printed all over the surface). I just finished listening to a program of yours. You challenged adults to 'do something' about the lonely children of our country. You exhorted Christian businessmen to hire mothers with attention to school hours, and pleaded for surrogates to show concern for a lonely one. You, in fact, put the responsibility on *everyone* except mothers.

"I speak from a very deep conviction of being a 'keeper at home.' I have not worked since I've been married. We've eaten beans sometimes, but I've never regretted not working. We live in a wicked, hedonistic society. I am home-schooling and raising my own children. If you are so soft on working mothers, how are you different from the world? Stand for Christ, and back off being a worldly-wise woman. Be an individual who makes a difference for Christ, not mammon."

Someone else recently counseled me to come down harder against working moms. I know that the traditional anti-working-mom approach would make my message more popular in some circles, but I simply can't be that hard. I can't "come down harder" on the working mom. Besides, it seems so many others in the Christian community are already applying themselves to that job. But, despite the outcry, more mothers are working than ever before.

We may not agree with her values.

We may feel she's abandoning her children.

We may resent the way the world pats her on the back.

But, for our Lord's sake, we dare not allow our differences, or our principles, to become a weapon that we hold against her. It's sin not to care, to withhold God's love—even for Christian principles. It's sin to refuse to address the needs of hurting children because you don't approve of how their mother spends her day. It's sin to withhold love from a woman because she's a working mom. God has entrusted his church with the care of those he loves. What's worse than Christian caregivers who abuse that trust, withhold God's love, for principle?

What's it like to be a working mom in the Christian community these days? One woman writes describing her frustrations this way: "I am a working mother, abruptly redirected by divorce and the economic pressure that follows. I am full of guilt and frustration. It seems the only words the Christian community has for us compounds our guilt and advises us to 'stay at home,' which we can't do. Can you help us?"

Most working moms feel that the Christian community doesn't care about them at all. They often see us as ones who "compound" their problems.

I wonder how Christ would respond to the working mom if he were walking on earth today? Would he feel comfortable with the attitudes that prevail in so many religious settings? We can get a clue from one biblical account. A crowd of the self-righteous and principled, the teachers of the law, dragged a woman to him by night. They were angry. They had caught her in her sin.

"Teacher, this woman was caught in the act of adultery. In the Law Moses commanded us to stone such women. Now what do you say?" (John 8:4).

Jesus said, "If any one of you is without sin, let him be the first to throw a stone at her" (John 8:7).

Notice that Jesus didn't say, "If any of you has not committed adultery, let him throw the first stone." Probably some of them could have stoned the woman on that basis. He said if any of you is without sin—without any sin—then you may accuse.

What would Jesus say today to the principled among us, the ones who have grown straight without growing compassionate, to the teachers of the "law," to the ones practiced in accusation and unfamiliar with compassion? Would he appreciate the way we well-meaning people are "standing up" for him? Would he pat us on our stiff little backs, congratulating us for our "deep convictions"? I don't think that would be his response.

I believe he might tell us to be aware of our own sins before we become too accusatory.

What sins? We're not abandoning our children! Not us "I dids" and "You should toos"!

We should throw stones only if we are without "any" sins. I take Jesus' words here very literally. It is his caution to religious communities whose self-righteous tendencies we, unfortunately, always have with us.

We should be careful of the sin of pride that makes it too easy to accuse the working woman of child abandonment while we polish our "keeper-at-home" medals. We should beware of the sin of indifference that allows us to write off the entire world, except ourselves, as "wicked and hedonistic." We should beware of "deep convictions" that harden our hearts in self-righteous unconcern for a world God loves.

Who cares about the working woman? Is she anything to you? Does your heart go out to her children in Christian compassion?

My husband recently had an experience that reminded me of how quickly our secure, comfortable worlds can be shattered. He was involved in a three-car accident that totaled his car. They had to pry him out of it, but he escaped with only a minor head injury and cervical strain.

Two days later he left for over a month of traveling to pastor's conferences, and I couldn't help thinking, in the loneliness of the moment, that if he had been killed in that car accident, I would not be looking forward to the day when he would again walk through our back door.

It may be just a heartbeat, a car accident, a fatal illness that redefines my life from a woman whose husband provides financially for her, to someone who has no one. Then I too would have to be a full-time working mom. How quickly everything can change!

During that month I thought a great deal about what it would be like to be a single parent. Our budget was unusually tight so I didn't have a cent to spend on "extras." That's what it's like for a lot of single moms every month. I realized the phone didn't ring as often with Steve gone. Mostly it rang for the boys. I was more tired at night from being the only one overseeing the chauffeuring, the cooking, the laundry, the homework, the piano practicing. I didn't have someone to help me debrief my day or to share my ideas and frustrations. Little things seemed to discourage me more. My spirits dragged around me like a shadow.

I thought of adding to the discouragement of that month the feelings of abandonment that so many divorced women feel.

I thought of adding the widow's grief to that list.

I added to the list the burden of financial insecurity that drives some married women to work.

I thought the world is a hard place.

I thought people who are principled but compassionless are apt to make it worse by becoming oppressors to those who don't meet their standards. Insisting that all mothers stay home, regardless of their individual circumstances or their ability to do so, is oppressive. Insisting that these women's children are no one else's responsibility is simply oppression.

Note these words from Scripture:

> Woe to those who make unjust laws, to those who issue oppressive decrees, to deprive the poor of their rights . . . making widows their prey and robbing the fatherless. What will you do on the day of reckoning, when disaster comes from afar? (Isa. 10:1–3)
>
> Religion that God our Father accepts as pure and faultless is this: to look after orphans and widows in their distress. (James 1:27)

Would God be displeased if Christians applied a spirit of mercy to working moms and their self-care children? If we are to be principled people, let's be principled in the spirit of love and mercy.

What is the Christian community's bottom line regarding working mothers? Yes, it's important to tell young mothers to stay home with their babies, but we must include the words: "if it's at all possible." Yes, it's important to realize that the emotional slack in children's lives needs to be addressed. But, our most important message is redemption and compassion. Do we care about bringing working moms and their children to the Lord? Do we offer Christ's love to the working mom and her self-care children in the same spirit that he asked us to offer his love to widows and orphans? Or would we rather beat them over the heads with our "deep convictions" until they're totally alienated from Christ and his church?

The old saying tells us that the way to a man's heart is through his stomach. I don't know if that's true, but I'm sure of this: The way to a working mom's heart is through her child(ren).

A working mom's children are her great concern. The Christian community needs to recognize that and quit characterizing her as a callous woman who puts as much distance between herself and her children as possible. I know that type exists, but generally most working moms are really torn by their situations. I know few full-time working moms who think they have the greatest life. Most are overworked, overstretched, overstressed, and underpaid. No one I know is saying it's as great as the magazines make it out to be.

Working women are hurting, and we need to care about that. But our position needs to go beyond understanding. We need to put our arms around their children and begin to woo the mothers to the Lord. Even the working mother who knows the Lord needs to experience the support and care of God's people. The "*I can'ts*" could particularly use some understanding compassion from the "*I dids!*" and the "*You should toos!*"

As the family structure of our society disintegrates through divorce and the feminization of the workplace, we can stand on the sidelines and bemoan the situation, or we can roll up our sleeves and get busy. These are days of great spiritual potential if we will get involved. Most of us Christians could have a vital ministry right in our own neighborhoods if we allowed the Lord to tenderize our hearts to the working mom and her children. Think of the potential for evangelism if Christians would capture this vision!

Who cares for the woman who leaves her children for the "glamour" of the workplace—to punch the cash register at a local discount store, to clean other people's houses, to serve as a waitress, to type, to nurse, to teach? Who cares for the woman who "does it all"? Who cares for the one who's so depleted at the end of the day that she may have little left over for her own children? Who cares for the woman who's been abandoned by a husband—or who sleeps with widow's grief in a double bed?

Who cares for today's working woman? Who cares for her kids? The community of believers needs fewer voices crying "I did!" and "You should too!" Let's try saying, "I care." And let's put our words where the working mom's heart is. Let's care for her by caring for her children.

It seems to me that the Christian community has enough people who are ready to "stand up for Jesus." Let's not just "stand up for Jesus." Let's do some of the "caring in the name of Jesus" that this world so desperately needs to receive.

FOURTEEN

The Serendipity Sisters

*No eye has seen, no ear has heard, no mind
has conceived what God has prepared for those
who love him.*

1 Corinthians 2:9

Throughout this book I've tried to give a realistic picture of what it means to overlook the "childishness" of someone else's child. I've said that children looking for love may not be model children. They may be more in the "some friend" category that we need to learn to accept.

But not all children fall into that category. Sometimes the children who need our love may be close to model children. They may be entirely lovable. In fact, I would say that's been our experience with our two "daughters," Sharon and Faith Hamilton.

We first met Sharon and Faith ten years ago when my husband, Steve, and I took a group of twenty-six students to Peru for a summer missionary trip. They are daughters of the Irish-English missionary couple with whom we stayed in Lima.

Their mother had requested that we bring a few things that she had picked out from the Sears catalog. So, although the Hamiltons paid for them, we came bearing gifts. Roller skates and new clothes, cake mixes and gelatin so common in America were unaffordable luxuries at the local prices. We were instantly elevated to hero status in the eyes of these unspoiled missionary children. It was Christmas in July.

I watched their mother, an enthusiastic sprite of an Englishwoman, unwrap the boxes we brought her, and I was amazed when she pulled out items to hear her declare, "Oh, I'll give this cake mix to Martha. She'll really enjoy it. And I'll give this packaged cereal to the Anderson kids. It's been a long time since they've tasted American cereal."

Joan and Robert Hamilton had been missionaries to the Indians of the Peruvian mountains for many years, living a life that had been stripped to its basics. They had allowed themselves few luxuries, little pampering. I affectionately nicknamed Joan "Mountain Woman" and enjoyed her pioneer missionary zeal for living. "Don't let Joan take you out walking!" everyone warned me. "She's impossible to keep up with when she's 'on the hoof!'" I spent the weeks eating the woman's dust as I followed her, entranced with this tough, enthusiastic missionary woman.

I learned she was legendary for her lack of fear. Someone told me how she caught a thief who had been robbing their home. He had chosen Sunday mornings to break into their home when he knew the family would be at church. Joan stayed home by herself the next Sunday, hiding in a cupboard, waiting for the thief to try again.

He did come back to break in.

But Joan was waiting for him. She emerged from her hiding place and caught the neighbor boy, whom she had suspected. Marching him to his parents, she announced, "Here is our thief!"

Another more serious incident found her alone in the house, having just stepped out of the bathtub, when she realized someone else was there. Two armed men pushed her into her bedroom and demanded all her silver and gold. "We are not rich!" she told them. "We only have a couple of rings and little pieces of jewelry."

As they continued to search the bedrooms for their loot, Joan escaped through a second-floor window. Breathing a prayer as she climbed a wall to escape, she managed somehow to land uninjured on the other side of the wall. From there she rushed across the street to a store and called the police.

I have been on a lot of mission fields, known a lot of missionaries, but "Mountain Woman" came closest to meeting the ideals of what a pioneer missionary woman should be like. I liked her spunky spirit. I enjoyed the way she laughed at life. I admired her greatly. When we said good-bye at the Lima airport that summer, I had no idea of how entwined our lives would become.

"Sharon and Faith are coming to the States for school, Sharon for college and Faith for high school. Would you be willing to be their legal guardians? It means signing forms for school, etcetera. We don't know that many people in the States."

We said "Sure!" and felt strangely matured in our role as guardians to two teenage girls.

Sharon came the first summer alone. The Hamiltons could afford to bring only one of the girls back to Peru for the summer, so Faith had gone back to see her parents since she was younger. It was the summer we moved to Illinois. My mother had recently died, and we were moving into my parents' house—vacant since their deaths. Brendan was six, Justin was three. Sharon was seventeen. It was as if the Lord provided a nanny for the Bell boys. She was good with the boys, and they, in turn, loved her. I don't think I would have gotten through that stressful summer of moving into my parents' home (still furnished with all their things) if it hadn't been for Sharon.

Both Sharon and Faith came back to Illinois for Christmas that year. It was Faith's first Christmas away from her parents. She was homesick and stayed in her bedroom by herself much of the time. For Christmas day my brother came with his family. We tried to be extra celebrative for the sake of the girls who were so far from home, and for our own sakes, this first Christmas without a living parent, but it just seemed to increase the sadness we were all feeling.

Finally the phone rang—long distance from Peru. *Now everything would be all right,* I thought. *The girls will have a nice long talk with their parents, and they'll feel much better.*

I could hear Sharon and Faith's excited voices in the stairwell. I imagined their mother's positive tone on the other end. I knew she had the ability to make them feel better just by talking to them.

The phone call ended after only three minutes. We waited for the girls to come join us in the living room, but instead we heard muffled crying in the stairwell.

A three-minute phone call can be a bittersweet experience—especially if it's the only one your parents can afford to make for a long time, especially if you're young and missing them terribly.

"Come here." Steve gently called them. They came into our living room. We made room on the couch for them between the couples and put our arms around them. We all cried that Christmas. My brother and I, still fresh in our grief and understanding too well what it means to miss parents, cried. Our spouses cried. I cried for the daughters, and I wondered if their parents were sitting near a phone in Peru, crying too.

But I knew that somehow everything was going to be all right. I knew then that we would commit ourselves to being "home" for these two girls. I shuddered to think how I paled in comparison to "Mountain Woman." I would probably find myself eating her dust, but somehow I would try to be a mother to these two teenage girls.

So since 1982, we've had the pleasure of their company at most Christmases and during summer vacations. I would say they have taught us the meaning of the word "unspoiled."

That first summer Sharon stayed with us in Illinois, she tried to find a ride back to college in Florida for the fall term, but she was unsuccessful. She could have asked us to pay for a plane ticket, but she didn't. Instead, she and my niece Melissa organized a bake sale. They baked seventy-five pies, and dozens of small loaves of spice breads, staying up all night before the sale. They baked in my sister's kitchen, as the Bell kitchen was in the middle of being remodeled. (My sister is a good sport. She spent the next week washing flour dust out of her kitchen cupboards.)

Standing on the corner in front of our home, they sold their homemade creations and earned not only enough money for a plane ticket back to college but also some money for a back-to-school shopping trip as well.

I remember another incident that taught us about being "unspoiled." One Christmas Eve we were all singing around the piano, when Steve noticed that Sharon was singing only the first verses of the carols. "Sharon," he said, "why aren't you singing the other verses? Can't you see them?"

"No, it's all blurry, but I know the first verses from memory!"

"Why didn't you tell us you were having problems seeing?"

"Well, I would have to have my eyes checked and maybe get new glasses, and we just can't afford it."

I remembered that this missionary family had rarely been to doctors because of the expense. I remembered the infre-

quent phone calls because of the lack of money. I remembered having to choose one daughter to come home because
there wasn't enough money to buy airline tickets for two. I
suddenly felt ashamed of the money I had spent on social
lunches and things I really didn't need.

"You are going to the eye clinic while you're here this
Christmas!" Steve insisted.

A pair of contacts and a pair of new glasses later (thanks
to financial help from our extended families), Sharon,
whom we discovered couldn't read the big "E" at the top of
the exam chart with her glasses off, was seeing again.

Through their high-school, college, and young-adult
years we were "there" during broken romances, changed
majors, getting a driver's license, an engagement, wedding
plans, and recently a new baby.

I no longer worry about being pale in comparison to their
wonderful mother, the "Mountain Woman." I've long ago
accepted that as fact. But I now know that as far as my relationship with her children goes, the important thing is to be
committed and to continue to "be there."

Someone has said that missionary children are the
unsung heroes of the mission field. I would say that's true,
but I would add that the mothers and fathers of missionary
children model a kind of heroism every time they have to
send one of their children away somewhere for education.
The Hamiltons have done it with a lot of style, a lot of grace.
Their sacrifice has gone unsung, unnoticed by nearly everyone except a few of us who have watched these personal
struggles closely.

I've learned a lot from this family by watching them.
They've done without the things most of us would consider
basics. And yet . . .

I've never heard a complaint.

I've never detected a whine in their voices.

I've watched them cheerfully do without.

Faith came into some money recently. "What are you going to do with your money, Faith? Do you want to go shopping for school clothes?" I asked.

"Oh, I thought I would send the money home to Mum and Dad. They could probably use it more than I need it right now. What would I spend it on? I have enough clothes," she responded.

I remembered her mother giving away the cake mixes we had brought for her. Like mother, like daughter.

Sometimes people will say to us, "Oh, you've done so much for those girls!" I want to say, "But we've received so much more than we've given!" But how would I explain what it means to us to see them cuddled up with our boys watching television together? How can I tell of all the things they've helped us do around this house from wallpapering to baby-sitting? Would they understand how far we've come in our comfortableness with each other if I told them this year Faith's anniversary card to us said, "Dear Mum and Dad . . . from the three of us Brendan, Justin, and Faithie." Would they understand what the phone calls that keep us connected mean or how much we value the perky voices that say, "Just wanted to hear your voices—just wanted to make sure you're okay."

Someone else's child doesn't always belong to an adult who's been derelict in their responsibilities. That someone else may be one who could easily leave the rest of us in the dust. Someone else's child may not be just that ragtag, problem kid from next door. Someone else's child may be someone who gives you much more than you could ever give back.

I have to laugh when I think about my dream in which I told the Lord that I would really like a baby girl—the one I anticipated finding on my front porch in a little pink basket. I dreamed that dream after the first summer Sharon came to live with us, before our "sad" first Christmas together. I believe the Lord knew the desires of my heart even before he heard the dream prayer that came from my unguarded subconscious. He obviously had already planned to fill that empty spot in my life.

I was way behind him, eating his dust.

He didn't give me just one baby girl, though. He gave me two beautiful daughters, raised to unspoiled loveliness by their missionary mother, the woman who then left them with us when the time came for her to send them away. God already had a plan in motion before I could even articulate my desires to him. He was way ahead of my plans for myself.

When did the Lord conceive his plan to put us together? Was it when we met each other on that summer missionary trip? Was it when my own mother died that the Lord decided to bless me by extending my family with Sharon and Faith? Or could it have been at some earlier point that he anticipated our mutual needs and decided we would be a good match?

I don't know the answers to those questions. I do sense that his hand has been involved in bringing about serendipitous blessings from things that initially seemed simply convenient. I had only planned to "be there" for the girls. I had no way of knowing that I would be the one on the receiving end. When I think of the weaving of our lives—an English missionary couple in Peru, a young couple in Illinois, and two teenage girls—I wonder at the beauty and intricacy of his good planning. In my wildest dreams I had dared to ask only for one daughter—he gave me two!

Some children, teenagers, or college students may need you to "be there" for them. You may be thinking of something as small and functional as having them over for a meal or going to lunch together. Be ready. God may have better plans for you than you have for yourself. He may be planning to bless you greatly—even more than you could imagine in your wildest dreams. He may already be leaving you and your earth-bound plans behind in the cloud of his holy dust. Look closely and follow that cloud! When the dust settles, you may find his blessing on your life.

FIFTEEN

Friend-of-Children Checklist

The point of having an open mind, like having an open mouth, is to close it on something solid.

G.K. Chesterton

Concern for children is admirable, but if lonely children are to be helped, we must move from concern to action. This checklist can help you position yourself as a friend of children.

* Develop a positive attitude. Believe in the difference one life can make. Begin to pray every day that the Lord will make you sensitive to the needs of the children where you live. Believe that he wants to address those needs through you.

* Study the chapter on the characteristics of a nurturer. What characteristics would describe you? What characteristics are you lacking? Begin to work toward becoming a more nurturing person in your relationships with children. You might take one characteristic that you admire and set aside a month to make it a habit in your life.

* Make a list of the children in your life. You may not even know their names at this point, but list them anyway. Beside their names, write a short note describing their life. Are their parents divorced? Is their mom working full time? Do the children have apparent problems: do they look unkempt; do they seem sad and overly quiet; do they whine or have difficulty making eye contact; do they get along with other children; do they just hang around by themselves at church or in the neighborhood? List the potential problems that may indicate their risk of growing up lonely, detached, or emotionally separated.

* Resolve to learn the names of the children in your life and begin always to address them by name when you're with them. This is a simple practice that is overlooked by 99 percent of the adult world. Greeting a child by name says, "You have value." I often add an affectionate nickname after I've gotten to know a child. Nicknames also say, "You're special." In fact it says, "You're so special that you need a special name." An old proverb I agree with says, "A child that is loved has many names."

* Prepare some standard conversation starters that will help you speak to children and bring them into the conversational group. Almost any question will do. You might notice their clothing and make a comment like, "Where did you get those neat shoes? Wish I had a pair like that!"

My husband has a line he likes to deliver, and it always gets quite a response from both boys and girls. "Are you married?" he asks in all seriousness. When they respond no to this adult silliness, then he asks them, "Why not?" We've heard some interesting responses to that one, but the old trick works. It gets them talking, and most children enjoy the attention.

* Convey "You have value" with appropriate ways of touching. It's sad in this day of child sexual abuse that many adults have become cautious and self-conscious about giving physical affection to children. But children still need an affirming touch from adults.

A squeeze around the shoulders is very acceptable, and other safe gestures can also convey affection. I realized this recently when I watched my husband drawing a marker tattoo on a friend's child's arm for Halloween. For ten minutes they worked in close proximity while Steve held the boy's arm and carefully drew what the boy had requested. We didn't know this child well, but the tattoo experience began a special trusting relationship.

If you can style or braid hair, you have a skill any little girl appreciates. This gesture conveys, "You have value. In fact, you have enough value that I'm going to help you look beautiful." Even working together on a project can foster a friendly intimacy that feels like emotional touching. It's part of the "being there" that so many children's relationships with their own parents lack. Touch and being together convey a sense of trust and belonging. It's missing in too many children's lives these days.

* Identify the adult barriers that have kept you from "being there" for children. What's keeping the children in your life at a distance? Do you have too clean a house, a competitive spirit for your own children that excludes others from your care, a prejudice against "childishness"? What is keeping you from meeting the needs of some nearby child? Begin to weed that attitude from your life for the sake of a little one who may desperately need you.

* Identify a particular child or children to whom you can begin to reach out with significant gestures. Remember it doesn't take a lot to impress a child. Carry gum to share or keep little snacks on hand for small visitors to your home. It may be that you can include this child in family activities, errands, and trips.

* Get to know the child's parents and let them know that you don't feel imposed on if the child spends a lot of time with you. Tell the parents the special qualities you've observed in their child. Report funny things their child has said. Try to build up the child's image to his or her parents. Find ways to say, "I enjoy your child. She's very special." This is important not only to diffuse any feelings of displacement the parents may feel but also to increase the child's home image by having someone else who thinks he or she is great.

* Tell the child the special things you've observed about him or her. You don't need to make things up. Every child has special qualities that you can help cultivate and encourage.

* "Be there" for that child. Inconvenience yourself if you must, but make the necessary adjustments in your life to address the needs for "belonging." Try to say no rarely. Help the child develop trust toward others through his or her feelings of being able to count on you.

* Pray for the Lord to make himself real in this child's life, and then be ready to point out indications of God's activity. "No, it wasn't just 'luck' that helped you find your keys. God cares about you and helped you find them." In this day of decreasing church attendance, you may be the only access some child has to God. It is no mere coincidence that this child has found a Christian adult with whom to connect.

Many things can be done on a more organized level to position yourself as a friend to children. Even if you don't have contact with any particular child right now, you may want to think about some of the following ideas so that you can model your lifestyle in a "pro-family" fashion.

* If you are in a position of influence or if you hire working mothers, consider giving them the option of working a more flexible schedule than nine o'clock to five o'clock. Many family problems, such as after-school childcare, could be alleviated if more women had the option of working during school hours instead of regular traditional office hours.

* We will be hearing more about job sharing for working mothers in the days to come, but it would be great to hear that this creative approach was occurring in places where Christians have influence over policy. I share my current job with another part-time writer. We both benefit by being able to work enough to take the sting out of our family finances, yet we still have time to be mothers. I believe our employer benefits by having two "great minds" applied to one job. This is a workable concept that can make everyone a winner.

* Consider organizing an after-school program for self-care children in your church. In many churches this is already happening. In some places a before-school program is being operated as well. The First Covenant Church in Portland, Oregon is meeting the need for children who are alone. Oregon law requires any child under ten to be attended. "Each school day morning a fifteen-passenger van leaves the church parking lot full of active grade-school children. In the afternoon it picks them up again and takes them to church. For several years the program has provided quality day care to these children whose parents work. 'Cov-

enant House' is fully licensed by the state of Oregon to serve up to thirty-five children. A committee within the church oversees the ministry, setting policies and hiring personnel. The parents pay a fee based on the number of hours the children are in the program. The church subsidizes Covenant House from its budget and fundraisers."[1]

* Investigate the possibility of volunteering your nurturing skills at your local grade school or as a Sunday school teacher or in an after-school Bible club. If you find nothing that you can get involved with, then start something yourself. Talk about the needs of children and mobilize people around you to address those needs.

These are all initial steps in becoming involved in children's lives. Some adults will move beyond these steps to more formal caring relationships, such as foster care and adoption. Some will specialize in caring for children with particular needs, such as those born with drug addictions or those with handicaps. We all differ in our capacities for nurturing and in our levels of involvement. Almost everyone can be involved in meeting children's needs on some level, however. The important thing is to become aware and then to get started. This is a job for the body of Christ, whether we are young, old, married, or single. We can all be friends to children. Let's begin today.

SIXTEEN

When One Little Old Lady Made a Difference

*Saints are people who make it easier for others
to believe in God.*

Nathan Soderblom

Life is so circular, full of repeating patterns and nuances. In some ways my story has come full circle. It began in the fifties with a lonely little girl and an elderly neighbor woman.

My life had begun to change when my family moved from our city apartment to Illinois Street in suburban Wheaton, Illinois. My parents had made a relieved exit from a city building layered with young families, to "a house of their own" in the suburbs. They moved for the good of their children. But to my disappointment, our new neighborhood had no children my age. My former city playmates were gone, and I became an "only child."

But that year held other changes. My baby brother, Craig Richard, was born. Mother was now a forty-year-old woman with two small children and an older child in grade school. Exhausted by the demands of a baby, an active toddler, and a school-aged child, she managed our home with an air of preoccupied busyness. My brother articulated his needs loudly and clearly, as all babies do. I couldn't find such an effective and acceptable method to express my needs. Through my brother's birth I learned what one often learns through the death of a loved one—that we are all ultimately alone in this life.

Displaced from the nurture of my mother, removed from the comfort of my friends, I began to move away from family, away from mother and brother, into myself. As a young child I began a journey that would continue into my young adult years. I took the first steps that would make me feel like a stranger to my own people. I began to watch the warm family circle from the fringes as if I were a detached observer. I backed away from them into a place of lonely isolation and wondered why they didn't come to rescue me or to pull me back inside their circle. They never realized how lost I had become. How could they? I was very young. I couldn't tell them of the loneliness I felt when I woke up; I didn't know the name for the feeling that haunted my days and gnawed at my heart when I lay in my bed at night. I knew I lived at 324 East Illinois Street, Wheaton, Illinois, but I also knew that nobody there knew me well. I was alone.

I would learn something else about life in those early years. With loneliness comes latitude. While I missed my mother's undivided attention, with a tinge of delight I realized that I now had much less adult supervision. I was a free agent. My family nicknamed me Valerie "B-Bomb" Beth Burton during those preschool, pre-civilized years on Illinois Street, and I got that name the old-fashioned way. I earned it!

I learned I could enjoy dumping sand in my hair for a long time before anyone told me to stop. I could be uninhibited in my backyard play. I could be a horse, an untamed backyard equine, a creature of both strength and beauty. Neighing, hooves slashing the air, dandelion mane flying in the wind, I was the leader of my imaginary herd. With courage, uncanny intelligence, and unbelievable speed, I eluded my human captors and set free those poor horses in bondage to human saddles and bits. Life was adventurous, dangerous; I was a "wild thing."

It's interesting to read my mother's thoughts she recorded about my childhood. I think she too may have sensed me slipping from her arms into a place where I became increasingly difficult to hold and hard to manage.

> I often think of Valerie at two
> when "Don't do this" and
> "Don't do that"
> meant "Do!"
>
> On counter and on windowsill
> she often tried her fledgling will—
> knew no subsequential fear
> though warned by parent, peer.
>
> When on some catwalk's edge I lean
> and risk some slough's dark algae-green
> do your arms stretch toward me
> as mine once did for Valerie?
>
> Unbridled yet—my human will—
> be Thou, O God, my Codicil.[1]

Actually, I often managed to terrify myself when my imagination became blurred with reality. The drumbeats of the nearby high-school marching band always sounded to me like the tom-toms of marauding Indians. I knew they were coming to get us, that my family would be in great danger, that it would be up to me to devise the scheme to save our scalps. This seemed like reality to me. Disaster was always just around the corner.

When life as a solitary wild thing wore thin, I would take a door-to-door tour of the neighborhood, begging food (with excellent results, to my mother's great embarrassment) before anyone missed me at home. I don't remember being hungry, but I do remember wanting to be with someone. I didn't know whom I was looking for, but I was driven to look for him or her in our neighborhood. I carried my loneliness from house to house hoping someone could take this aching burden from my heart. I didn't know how to correct my problems relating to my own family. I would have to find another. Where was the soul-mother who would welcome me in? Where was the understanding father who would help me find my lost self? Where was the warm family circle to which I belonged?

I'm not exactly sure how old I was when I began to be interested in the "witch" next door. She was the oldest woman on the street. Using a cane, she maneuvered her bent, darkly clothed body through her backyard. I was prejudiced against her age. I knew about witches. I had heard of Hansel and Gretel! I spied on her from hiding places, and if she saw me, she never spoke a word.

Repulsion mixed with attraction, and one day I found myself climbing the stairs of her gingerbreaded front porch. Slowly sounding out the words, I read the sign that announced in faded ink and large print—KNOCK ONCE AND COME IN. *This is too easy. It must be a trap to get me!* I thought. But loneliness and curiosity won out over fear; I knocked once and walked in—one step.

She came to the door through a room of worn Victoriana. Mauve and cream wallpaper framed her approaching form. An eternity seemed to pass between each step as this aged specter labored her way toward me. I've tried to remember her face, but it's lost to my memory. I've wondered how that could possibly happen. Perhaps because she flooded my senses with so many vivid impressions, the ordinary form of her face faded behind more imposing details in the vault of my childhood memories. For instance, I clearly remember her hands. I was at eye level with the blue veins that wound through an intriguing landscape of wrinkled, transparent skin.

In time I became a regular visitor to the old "witch's" house. She wooed me with shredded wheat, popcorn balls, and homemade gingerbread. I learned to call her Grandma Wheaton. I never remember being asked to leave; she simply integrated me into the activities of her day. When she became tired, we napped together, playing a game called "Let's see who can go to sleep the quickest." I knew this game lacked the essential element of fun, but my competitive spirit compelled me to try to win. When naps were over, I would always claim the victory, announcing "I won! I won!"

No one else competed for Grandma Wheaton's time. I was the object of her full attention. And she had my full attention when she began to tell her stories. She was legendary in our small town for the volumes of poems and stories she had committed to memory. It was an empty time of life for the old woman and me, but her stories filled our days. Some were stories from her life. She told the story of her mother, who had been killed when a train's cowcatcher had snagged the hoop of her skirt, pulling her under its grinding wheels and throwing her infant child, Grandma Wheaton's brother, onto the smoke stack. Home as Grandma Wheaton had known it was no more. She would go through life motherless.

She told the story that went with the faded picture of the sailor-suited boy, her child, who had died in an epidemic when he was twelve years old. Motherless and childless, she was familiar enough with loneliness to recognize the symptoms in me. I particularly remember her stories about orphans. How I felt for those children who lived in alleys and begged for food in city streets! Too well I understood those pathetic children who grew wild in their hopelessness.

Grandma Wheaton's stories seemed incredibly sad to me, but I sensed a deeper theme to all of her tales. It was faith in God. It was the theme of her life. She believed that Jesus would fit all the lonely holes in our lives with himself. Her lifetime of pain was made sweet by her unshakable faith. As she spun her stories for me, she filled up the empty places of my life with her faith. I, a wild child who had believed only in Indian drums and the certain dangers of life, now knew there was an answer to my loneliness. Jesus loved me. I believed.

I think of Grandma Wheaton with great tenderness today. How blessed I was that she was open to being found "with child" in her advanced age. How blessed I was that she recognized my alienation and searched for my lonely soul until she had brought it to its only real home—Jesus. What a wonderful thing to be included in the smallest family circle on Illinois Street. She loved me, a child not of her womb. She loved me, a child of daily inconvenience, and I belonged. As for Grandma Wheaton, sometimes I wonder about her. Did she ever laugh Sarah-like at this untamed remedy for old-age loneliness? Had God chosen for some reason to wait until her advanced age to answer an earlier Hannah-prayer for a child? I wish I knew.

One thing I know. Lonely children live in every neighborhood. They are alienated from their families by divorce and other family circumstances. They awake every day engulfed by sad loneliness. They don't know the names for their feelings. They don't know how to talk about it. They come from secular as well as Christian homes, where they feel unknown.

They come from homes destroyed by divorce, from homes where adults are consumed by their own problems. They're both latchkey kids and kids whose mothers and fathers are too preoccupied to give them more than token attention. They're the unfavorite daughter or the quiet, melt-into-the-wall son.

They're left to forage emotionally, to seek nurture in strange places, to eat well-being crumbs from the leftovers in homes more comfortable to them. Others neglect them, and these children harm themselves through their own inability to relate to the significant people in their lives. Unmothered, unfathered, they seek a soul-parent who will find their lost selves and bring them to an emotional and spiritual home. They're looking for the door with the sign that announces, "KNOCK ONCE AND COME IN—and stay as long as you would like!"

It seems to me that God allowed me, a child from a home with two parents who loved me, to feel the aching burden of such loneliness. Perhaps he allowed me to be impressed with enough of that sort of pain so that I would never forget. That remembered suffering has motivated me to try to give children a voice through my writing. I hope that you've heard them and that these voices will begin to take names and form faces where you live.

I thank God for little old ladies who give the time to make a difference in our lives. I thank God for allowing all of us to have some pain in our growing. It's remembered pain that makes us willing to carry someone else's hurts. I'm praying that the Lord will never let me forget how that pain felt when some small presence now seems just a little too constant. I want to be haunted by that aching loneliness every time I'm tempted to send a child home for the sake of my own convenience. I want to remember through my old age when my wrinkled skin becomes the object of some child's awe. I want to begin now to be a little old lady who makes a positive difference for others.

May the Lord remedy my old age as he has my middle years with the company of someone else's child. May I be ready to answer affirmatively the question, "Are you my mother?" when nobody's children drag their loneliness to my house. May the small space of my life be filled with an overflowing of believing. May it spill over to the lonely spaces of those small ones for whom you greatly care.

I tried to see Grandma Wheaton after we had moved from Illinois Street. I rode my bike across town to our old neighborhood. I was ten. The sign no longer hung on the door. I walked in, but the Victorian wallpaper was gone. Someone else was living in Grandma Wheaton's house. She was gone. I couldn't believe no one thought it was important that I should know what had happened to my friend. I never said good-bye or thank you. I must have raised a few eyebrows that day as I sat on the gingerbreaded front porch of strangers and cried.

Those tears have been gone for many years now. Gone too is the wild child driven by loneliness. I could easily forget they ever existed. But I have not forgotten my friend or how she filled my life on Illinois Street with a believing that has satisfied my loneliness for a lifetime.

Could it be that the Lord would begin to make his people sensitive to the crying needs of the children who live in their own neighborhoods? Who is the champion for children? Who will be Grandma Wheaton, Grandpa Wheaton, Mother Wheaton, Father Wheaton to the lonely ones in your neighborhood? Who will have an open door policy that announces, "KNOCK ONCE AND COME IN—and stay as long as you would like"? Who will fill the empty places in their souls with believing? Who will share their lives, their homes, their food, and their faith with these lonely ones?

Lord,

Shake us from our complacency and break our hearts for these your children. May we feel the pain you feel over these lonely and lost ones. And may that pain motivate us to a changed lifestyle that is lovingly inclusive of these ones for whom you greatly care.

Amen

SEVENTEEN

Spiritual Healing

I bandage, God heals.

Ambroíse Paré

During Molly's childhood, her parents went through a divorce. We've shared Molly's grief over the divorce of her parents. It spilled over into our kitchen and living room in a summer of sorrow.

"I used to have a dream of living in a happy family where we were all friends. That's all smashed—it will never be for me!" she cried.

"You're a part of our family. We will always have a special place for you in our home." I told her.

Out of her insecurity she asks me questions: "You and Steve are never going to get a divorce, are you?"

"Never!" I assure her. Sometimes I'm slow to read between the questions.

"Do you think you'll ever move away from this house?"

"Oh, I don't know. Maybe someday after the boys grow up we'll move to a smaller place."

A long pause. "Well, if you move away when I'm away at college, be sure you tell my mom so I can find you."

So that's what she's getting at! "Molly, when you're a mommy with darling little babies of your own, I want to see you with your own happy family. You're about the closest thing to a daughter I'll ever have!"

Because of the divorce, it was Molly's dark summer. She struggled with adult issues she couldn't possibly understand. Weighed down with rejection and grief, she wouldn't speak to her parents' counselor, turning her back rather than facing him in an act of defiance against combined adult forces.

"Would Molly like to go with the boys and me to North Carolina for a week this summer?" I asked her mother.

She agreed, so late one night on my first fourteen-hour drive without my husband, I drove to a favorite family place nestled in the mountains and forests, with two children of my womb and one of the Lord's choice.

Deep into the starlit night my boys deserted their Mother-watch to sleep. Molly and I were alone.

Leaning over the car seat and making eye contact in the rearview mirror, she began, "You're like a counselor to me. I understand how I feel about things when I talk to you. No, you're really more like my second mother." I smiled at this new-to-her revelation.

"I have something to tell you," she continued. "I haven't told anybody yet. This summer when I went to the camp your boys go to, I asked Jesus into my heart."

I stayed quiet, but my heart had taken a leap.

"I was so unhappy this summer. But now I'm not. I'm really happy."

"Oh, Molly, I'm so thrilled for you. What a difference this is going to make in your life!"

"Yeah, I want to be a missionary to Saudi Arabia!"

"Saudi Arabia! Where does this kid get this stuff?" I croaked inwardly. I imagined her parents keeling over from this bit of news. Outwardly I said, "Wow, isn't that something!" Watch out, Saudi Arabia!

At the North Carolina place we rendezvoused with a dear friend from Florida and her young son. Along the way we picked up a girl companion for Molly—Muffy. And so the house was full of children. We spent wonderful days in the creek and in the woods, nights by a fire with children playing board games.

We managed to quiet the children every other night but late on one particular night the mothers regressed to their own childhoods, laughing and carrying on in the master bedroom. "Shhhh!" the children chastened. "You're keeping us awake!" We tried, but found ourselves captives to the silliness of the late hour.

Then we heard the little voice. It was quiet at first. We strained to hear it.

"I love you, Lord, and I lift my voice to worship you, Oh, my soul, rejoice . . ."

"Who's singing?" I asked my equally puzzled and suddenly quiet friend Arnette. "It's got to be one of the girls. It's coming from their room. It's got to be Muffy!" I say. "Molly doesn't know any church songs."

"Kum-ba-yah, my Lord. Kum-ba-yah . . ."

The voice was pure and incredibly sweet, and we were all hushed. Soon, however, Arnette got up to identify our serenader and came back with the news. "It's not Muffy singing; she's asleep. It's Molly. Molly's singing!"

"Camp songs. She's singing camp songs!" I exclaimed sitting up board-straight in bed. The voice grew stronger in recognition of our muted appreciation. "Someone's praying, Lord. Kum-ba-yah . . ."

The voice took care to match pitch with the melody. Like a child taking first steps, it was careful, slow, then gained in joyful confidence. This child-voice carried us Godward and wrapped our cabin in awed worship. It felt like prayer. There was a sense of holiness with us. The night was pure.

"Take joy, my King, in what you hear. May it be a sweet, sweet sound in your ear."

Praise filled the night. Outdoors, a frog chorus accompanied the singer with a rhythmic chant. My heart leaped wildly heavenward. "I can't believe it's Molly, Lord. What an incredible thing has happened here!" The cabin was hushed, quiet, children and mothers all silenced, breathing quietly. It was a night to remember.

That summer I watched a spiritual healing before my eyes. This work was separate from my own; it was the grace of God extended to a lonely, grieving child. His love will never desert her or reject her or move away.

I think of other children like Molly. Some are adults now, but they continue to drag the loneliness and sadness of their inner child hopelessly into their adult years. I read their sad words:

> I was like the child, Jason, you talk about—having to find my sense of belonging and sense of home outside of my own. As a child I felt lonely, sad, and forgotten much of the time. It was like I was invisible; like no one could see me, because no one ever paid any attention unless I was in trouble. I still struggle with the aftermath and havoc it wreaked on my self-esteem.

My heart goes out to you, friend, but human compassion alone will not satisfy you for long. God provides a spiritual healing for children of all ages. It is more than any parent, natural or surrogate, can ever offer you. Let God love you. Let your inner child crawl up on Jesus' lap and experience the love that can heal your insecurities, your loneliness, and your pain. Your heavenly Father embraces you with acceptance and belonging. He is your soul Father, your emotional center, your true home.

Once we allow God to love us, then we can put our own arms around our child-selves and love that inner child. I love the "wild child" of Illinois Street with a deep understanding for her life situations. My mother-self has taken Valerie "B-Bomb" Beth Burton with her sand-filled dandelion hair, her off-the-wall behavior, her searching neighborhood visitations, and nurtured her to emotional health. I laugh at her, I enjoy her, but I never cry for her anymore. I accept her, I understand her life situation not as a hurting child, but as a whole adult. God, my soul Father, loves and accepts my wild-child self. I simply follow his example.

I know that our child-selves search tenaciously for healing. Even when our adult lives seem to be going all right, the wounded inner child keeps saying, "I hurt." If you suspect your child-self is dragging its pain into your adult life, then it's time to learn to accept the circumstances of your childhood without shame and go on to health and wholeness. You can remember your suffering without pain. It can even become a positive force in your life as you let it motivate you to care for those who have no sense of belonging, those who are nobody's children.

It's time to sing your holy song in the dark night of your soul. You are someone's child and well loved. Abandon your sadness to spiritual joy, and be healed. Listen to the bonds of loneliness drop from you as you come to your true spiritual home. Leave your solitary confinement; come to your place of belonging. Sing your song of freedom, of wholeness, of joy:

O for a thousand tongues to sing
My great Redeemer's praise,
The glories of my God and King,
The triumphs of his grace!

Jesus! The name that charms our fears
That bids our sorrows cease,
'Tis music in the sinner's ears,
'Tis life and health and peace.

He breaks the power of canceled sin,
He sets the prisoner free;
His blood can make the foulest clean;
His blood availed for me.

Hear Him, ye deaf;
His praise, ye dumb,
Your loosened tongues employ;
Ye blind, behold your Savior come;
And leap, ye lame, for joy.

My gracious Master and my God,
Assist me to proclaim,
To spread through all the earth abroad,
The honors of thy name. Amen.

Charles Wesley

"What does Molly mean when she says she asked Jesus
into her heart?" her mother asked one night.

"Oh, it's wonderful. It means that when your earthly father deserts you, your heavenly Father comes and puts his
arms around you and loves you. It means you never have to
be lonely or empty again." She seemed reassured. I wondered if she had heard about Saudi Arabia.

"Well, that sounds okay, I guess. Molly has a very pretty
voice, don't you think? Sort of folksy," Molly's mom mused.

"Yes, she does." I smile to think of the sweet incense of her song-prayers filling their home.

"I guess what I'm saying, Valerie, is that I want to give Molly to you as your spiritual daughter."

I'm amazed at these words, and my heart goes out to this friend of mine. I want to tell her that Jesus waits to love wives abandoned by husbands, just as he loves little girls abandoned by their fathers. But I sense it's too soon for that message, and that may be Molly's special job. I am just a piece of this puzzle, as was the old woman who loved me to Jesus, and someone before her no doubt who took her to heart when she was a child grieving for a mother lost forever beneath the wheels of a train. I am simply part of a long line of ones who have received love and in return loved other people's children. I imagine in time Molly will also be a part of that plan, maybe even in Saudi Arabia!

Therapists who work with unbonded, detached children find the healing process slow and often illusive. Many who specialize in "attachment therapy" hold little hope for the worst cases if these children fail to receive help before adolescence. But even in the midst of pessimistic alarm, therapists are still nodding in the direction of a spiritual healing to address our needs to belong, to be attached, to be bonded. Magid and McKelvey, authors of *High Risk, Children Without a Conscience,* mention it almost in passing, "But a true religious experience has been known to go beyond words. The spiritual message of love and redemption is emotionally charged and often experienced in an unforgettable manner. When this spiritual therapy works, the person becomes 'attached' to God."[1]

Here's the beautiful truth. God offers "belonging" to us all. We can never be too hopeless or beyond his ability to heal. Attachment to God can be experienced at any age. Our sense of belonging, of being Somebody's child, grows as we learn to trust him, as we learn to let him love us, as the reality of his care for us becomes a surety in our lives. This "spiritual therapy" begins with an initial trust experience—salvation, being born again, conversion, new life in Christ. Call it what you will, it means saying yes to God's offer of a new beginning. Once we come to God in childlike fashion and begin to relate to him as our well-intentioned Father, then the healing can begin.

Lonely children can benefit from a spiritual attachment to God, but adults, too, can allow their damaged child-selves to receive healing for the grown person. God's intention for us is a spiritual familial healing. He offers us sonship, daughtership. He offers us the deepest emotional belonging known to humanity. "You did not receive a spirit that makes you a slave again to fear, but you received the Spirit of sonship. And by him we cry, *Abba,* Father'" (Rom. 8:15).

Experts may not understand how it works. Perhaps that is why it often receives only a tip of the hat from them. But that it works they cannot deny. Those of us who understand attachment to God, who have experienced spiritual healing, and who owe our emotional health to it, must keep articulating its message of forgiveness, acceptance, and belonging. We need to model that hopeful message in the way we accept, and yes, love, hurting children—or adults whose inner child is still yearning to belong. It is the most hopeful message for people becoming increasingly detached in their person and family relationships.

I'm haunted by the tragic possibilities predicted for children and teenagers if their attachment needs aren't addressed. Words like the following chill me: "Social workers point to an enormous psychological problem in our society: many young people have never experienced a deep psychological attachment to anyone. They do not know how to love and be loved. The need to be loved translates itself into the need to belong to someone or something. Driven by their need, these young people become the victims of cults, of peer group pressure, of fads, in short, of any mass movement at hand. They will do anything to belong."[2]

The question we need to ask is: What am I willing to do to help a child "belong"?

I'm praying for this generation of children. Without intervention I sense they are in peril. I dream of a day when there will be enough sensitivity to their pain that they will be reached by communities of understanding adults. Even so, many children will never find satisfaction for those longings. Yet there will be some who will be drawn into warm family circles of caring Christian homes. There are wonderful stories to be told of the difference someone made in their lives. There are memories to be made, yearnings to be met, lives to be shared, spaces to be filled with believing.

It is a dream not out of our reach or beyond possibility. You and I can work to make this a reality for more and more children in our day.

Until then, I leave you with a blessing. Although admittedly it is a mixed one, it is my prayer for you. I give it to you with compassion for your life struggles and with joy for what the Lord will do for nobody's children through you.

May your porch be the refuge of someone else's child.
May your cookie jar know many small hands.
May your life be inconvenienced with nobody's child.
May you compassionately share the pain of a lonely child.
May your life-song be one that proclaims joy and belonging to all who need a home.
May your life overflow with believing to an empty child.
May you be known as a friend of children.
And may you experience your Lord's great pleasure when he thinks on you.

Epilogue

There have been many changes on Prairie Street since I first started writing and speaking about the children who lived with me there. The children have grown up and I—well, I am no longer a young mom, but a mother in her middle years. We are aging!

Now Prairie Street is the home of teenagers. Cars have replaced big wheels. The kids no longer move as a pack but have individuated their lives. The older ones have already gone to college, and others have moved to more upscale neighborhoods as their parents' careers progressed. But I suspect that in each of their hearts Prairie Street—that kids' paradise—will always be home.

Jason, my dark-haired intruder, is now eighteen. He and Brendan will graduate from high school in a few weeks, and I am already feeling separation anxiety for them both. They are still tight friends. Their friendship has survived having crushes on the same girls, competition for grades, and other misunderstandings along the way. At every possible fork in the road, they have chosen to work it out and remain friends. I am proud of their relationship and glad they have each other.

A couple of nights ago sort of captured our living together on Prairie Street. I experienced it with a sense of great blessing in my life. Early in the evening I sat on the

couch with Brendan and told him of my feelings of separation anxiety about his leaving home for college. He
laughed—I managed to smile. I know he is ready, eager
even, to move on with the next exciting and challenging
phase of his life. He is anticipating the future. I am remembering the past.

I know he can't understand my sadness at an end to a
personal era in my life. I hardly understand it myself. But I
am aware that our lives are changing. He is needing me less
and less. He laughs at my sentimental feelings—oh heartless
charmer! But in a gesture of compassion, he puts his arm
around me, and I rest my head on his shoulder. We capture
a few moments of pure togetherness. Without speaking or
moving, we silently listen to beautiful classical guitar music
from the stereo. I make a determined effort to capture this
moment in my memory bank. "Remember this forever,
Valerie!" an interior voice whispers to me. I am so blessed!

Later, Jason blows in. We sit on the stairs and talk. Brendan joins us fresh from the shower and still wrapped in a
towel. We lounge across the stairs, where our bodies have in-
formally dropped. What a strange group: two young men—
Jason sprawled on the landing while our cat, TarBaby,
expresses her undying love for him; and Brendan, still dripping but pausing for a while to talk—and me, an undeniably
middle-aged woman! It's boy talk. We joke and laugh at each
other. They talk about girls. I listen and laugh at their
descriptions. It's easy and comfortable and natural. At such
moments life is great.

Later, after the boys have cleared out and moved on with
their agenda for the night, Molly drops over on her way to
a youth-group activity. Life is an emotional roller-coaster
when you're fifteen and in the full throes of hormonal
pubescent life.

"How do I look?" she asks nervously.

"You look great!" I respond.

"Really? You're not just saying that? Cause there's this new guy at church—"

"Really. I love that color on you. You look wonderful!"

She's reassured. She's in and out, ready to charm and conquer. The guy probably won't know what hit him.

What I would have missed if I had closed my heart to these special children. Their friendship today is the fruit of those early years of "being there." The crumbs of bread I cast into the neighborhood waters have returned to me so many times over! It's all worth it.

Jason and Molly are spiritual pilgrims. Sometimes they walk backward, but to this point, we've watched as God has always broken through and turned them around.

Jason applied to a Christian college this year and was asked to describe his home life. He showed us his application, and I was surprised by the way he handled that question. "I do not spend much time at home. But I would like to tell you about the family where I have grown up—the Bells. I spend most of my time at my best friend's house. He has encouraged me to walk with God and challenged my faith when I have almost given up. Let me tell you about the Bells . . ."

It was the greatest compliment we have ever received as a family.

And then there's Molly. Her loyalty is amazing to me. She is a true friend. She has her highs, and frighteningly, she also has her lows. But every time she stumbles or falls, she comes back and is more established spiritually than ever.

Her mother and I talk. Surprisingly, she isn't intimidated by Molly's relationship to me. She is spiritually supportive, if not totally understanding. I tell her she is in the spiritual birth canal. She laughs. We both agree it has taken a couple of mothers to get this unusual child raised. We both love Molly. In my heart I feel she was fortunate to have us both.

Molly gave me a card for my birthday this year. It was so sweet, I asked her for permission to share it with you.

Valerie—

This is a very late birthday card—also a thank you for all of the talks, prayer, and help you have spread to me over the years. Not to mention wisdom. You have meant so much to me. I will always regard you as a second mom.

I can use your prayer still. I am going through a tough time, but I know that God will help me.

Thank you for everything.

I love you.

Always,

Molly

Her precociousness has developed into a word giftedness. We always suspected she was bright. These days she is writing poetry in a spiritual journal. I asked her if I could include an excerpt in this last chapter. The following is what she wanted you to know and remember about her at this point in her fifteen-year-old life:

Indigo

The sky,
flawless and clear
shimmering indigo
outlines the arms of our Savior.

Our Lord—outstretched
calling to the lost,
offering all he has,
asking only for belief
and promising the rest will follow.

Accepting guarantees only the best.
He offers everlasting bliss.

Once I accepted his gift,
life seemed so changed
so bright.

The iridescent sunlight of God
shone through my eyes.
Comfort and understanding,
truth and trust,
love and compassion,
eternity in his perfect presence.

Why would someone refuse?
Life may not be perfect.
Sometimes trials and tribulations arise—
but to know you always have a friend,
someone to confide in,
trust in,
and whose eyes are always looking lovingly on you.

I can't imagine anything more perfect
more wonderful!

> I look up to my God
> sitting on a cloud of fleece
> amidst the indigo-colored sky
> and my heart rests.

Well said, Molly. Amen!

My heart also rests, believing that God who has begun a good work in these children will complete it. My only regret as I look back on those years of high-kid traffic was that I wasn't more aggressive in reaching out. Looking back, and realizing the difference this has made for Molly and Jason, I only wish I had opened my heart wider, included more children regularly, and held on more tightly through the teen years.

My prayer for myself, and for you as well, is that we will be sensitive to the Mollys and Jasons all around us. Whether you are in the Kool-Aid Mom years of life, or you're closer to the Grandma Wheaton stage, I know you can make a difference for someone nearby. We can't afford to retire from this kid business.

The overwhelming evidence points to a frightening fact: Satan wants this generation of children. I believe that to my core! Just look at the statistics, and you have to be aware that evil is making significant inroads in the child-world. But I am aware of another truth: God wants them more!

When the smoke of this cultural battle clears, and the evidence is compiled concerning this generation of children, my hope is that out of the brimstone will arise the Molly stories, the Jason tales, the children God redeemed out of the ashes of destroyed lives. I pray it will be his day and that the evil plans for this group of children will go down in defeat because of neighborhoods like Prairie Street and neighbors like Grandma Wheaton and children like Molly and Jason to tell the stories of God's grace and redeeming goodness!

Let down the drawbridge! Throw open the doors of your heart! Molly and Jason are parked on the porch of your home. Will you let them in?

Notes

Chapter 3: Bless the Beasts and the Children

1. Amy Carmichael, from *Toward Jerusalem* (Fort Washington, Pa.: Christian Literature Crusade, 1936).
2. Arthur Unger, "ABC Probes Foster Care," *The Christian Science Monitor*, 30 August 1988: 20.
3. Barbara Dafoe Whitehead, "Dan Quayle Was Right," *The Atlantic* (April 1993): 47–84.
4. *Good Morning America* segment "Taking Control" report on financing daycare.
5. Marilyn Elias, "Alienation and Stress Afflict Latch Key Youths," *USA Today*, 6 September 1990: 1D.
6. "Children Beware," *USA Today*, 5 January 1993: 12A.
7. Howard Howe II, "The Prospect for Children in the United States," *Phi Delta Kappan*, 68, no. 4 (November 29, 1986): 191.

Chapter 4: Self-Care Children

1. Owen Seaman, "In a Good Cause," *Lotus Buds* (Madras, India: SPCK, 1926), vi.
2. Bob Greene, "Finding a Child Looking for Love," *Chicago Tribune*, 8 March 1988.
3. Martin O'Connell and David E. Bloom, "Juggling Jobs and Babies: America's Child Care Challenge." Report published by the Population Reference Bureau, Inc.
4. Robert Trotter, "Project Day-Care," *Psychology Today* (December 1987): 34.
5. Ibid.

6. Ellen Gray and Peter Coolsen, "How Do Kids Really Feel About Being Home Alone?" *Children Today* 16, no. 4 (July–August 1987).

Chapter 5: Are You My Mother?

1. P. D. Eastman, *Are You My Mother?* (New York: Random House, Inc., 1960).
2. Foster Cline, "Understanding and Treating the Severely Disturbed Child" (Evergreen, Co.: Evergreen Consultants in Human Behavior).
3. Ken Magid and Carole A. McKelvey, *High Risk: Children Without a Conscience* (New York: Bantam Books, 1988), 5.
4. Vera Fahlberg, "Attachment and Separation: Putting the Pieces Together" (Michigan Department of Social Services, 1979), DSS Publication 429.
5. Ibid.
6. Magid and McKelvey, 59.
7. Karl Zinmeister, "Hard Truths About Day Care," *Reader's Digest* (October 1988): 89.
8. The National Commission of Working Women's 1986 "Child Care Fact Sheet," Washington, D.C.
9. Jay Belsky, "The 'Effects' of Infant Day Care Reconsidered," *Early Childhood Research Quarterly.*
10. Zinmeister, 90.
11. J. Guidubaldi and J. D. Perry, "Divorce, Socioeconomic Status, and Children's Cognitive-Social Competence at School Entry," (American Orthopsychiatric Association, Inc., 1984), 459.
12. Burton White, "Should You Stay Home with Your Baby?" *American Baby* (October 1985): 27–28, 30.
13. Fahlberg, 7.

Chapter 6: A Heart Visitation

1. Dianthia Gilmore's story was published in the *Cleveland Plain Dealer*, 31 July 1988: 4-B.

Chapter 9: Spiritual Dreamers, Holy Schemers

1. Rusty Benson, "The Greenhomes Solution," *The PCA Messenger,* June 1988. For more information about Greenhomes America, write P.O. Box 17165 Memphis, TN 38187-0165.

Chapter 10: My God, My Neighbors, My Isaacs

1. Richard Conniff, "Families That Open Their Homes to the Sick," *Time* (December 5, 1988): 12.

Chapter 15: Friend-of-Children Checklist

1. Allan F. Johnson, "Covenant House: A Latch-Key Ministry," *The Covenant Companion* (October 1989): 12.

Chapter 16: When One Little Old Lady Made a Difference

1. Wilma Burton, *I Need a Miracle Today, Lord* (Chicago: Moody Press, 1976): 30.

Chapter 17: Spiritual Healing

1. Ken Magid and Carole A. McKelvey, *High Risk: Children Without a Conscience* (New York: Bantam Books, 1988): 223.
2. Albert LaLonde, *Quotable Quotations* (Wheaton, Ill.: Victor Books, 1985): 38.